Suits plus Creatives

A Guide to Collaborating and Communicating Across the Advertising Agency Divide

JOSEPH B. RADDING

Melvin & Leigh, Publishers

IRVINE, CALIFORNIA

Suits plus Creatives
A Guide to Collaborating and Communicating Across the Advertising Agency Divide

Published by Melvin & Leigh, Publishers
6 Curie Court
Irvine, CA 92617

orders.melvinleigh@cox.net
www.melvinleigh.com

Cover and interior design by Joseph B. Radding

ISBN: 978-0-99730846-4

Printed in the United States of America on mixed recycle paper

Visit our home page at www.melvinleigh.com

CONTENTS

FOREWORD

It's been said there are no original stories. More accurately, all the original stories have already been told and are just re-hashed versions of familiar tales. Even the noble bard himself, William Shakespeare, was a literary thief, "stealing" all but one of his famous and timeless works (for the curious, that original work was *The Tempest*). Take the Old Testament story of the Great Flood. It was actually first presented in the poem, "Epic of Gilgamesh"—1,000 years before Noah made the scene! Anyway, you get the idea ...

But a funny thing about stories—just because they may share similarities, it doesn't mean they can't be original. Culture, societal events, new ways to connect and, more importantly, imagination can reshape a story's perspective in a deeply emotional and relatable way for the reader or viewer.

I read a blog recently that demonstrated this theory by posing the following scenario regarding the identity of a story's hero:

"A young orphan who is being raised by his aunt and uncle receives a mysterious message from a stranger (a non-human character), which leads him on a series of great adventures. Early on, he must receive training to learn skills that are seemingly superhuman. Along the way he befriends loyal helpers, specifically a guy and a gal who end up falling for each other. His adventures lead him to a dark and evil villain who is terrorizing everyone and everything that our hero knows and loves — the same villain who killed his parents." *

If you haven't already noticed, two of the most famous, prolific, and incidentally, award-winning tales of our time turn out to be based on the same idea: Harry Potter and Star Wars!

The creative approach to telling familiar stories is the basic tenet of successful and effective brand communications and, hence, this book. But the success of any marketing effort does not rest on the laurels of the Creative Director alone (as much as they might believe that!).

* Melissa Donovan, founder and editor of www.writingforward.com

To coin a phrase, it takes an entire marketing team to ensure that what is delivered is not "creative for creativity's sake," but rather a strategic solution that will resonate with the target audience, open the door for brand discovery, and ultimately, compel a change in thought or behavior.

I first met Joe Radding over 20 years ago when we were both working at the same agency—he as a Creative Director and I as the Account Team leader. During my initial meeting with him I learned that he was an actor on the side, could wield a real sword, and was a card-carrying member of the Society for Creative Anachronism (look it up—it's fascinating!). More importantly, I remember being impressed with this multi-faceted individual and his lack of stereotypical "creative ego"; he was an interesting guy who intensely listened to multiple and sometimes opposing points of view, constantly asking the right questions, and being able to pivot on a creative dime when necessary. Challenge the status quo? Joe viewed that as simple routine. Despise ignorance? Yep, he did that too—all in the name of great stories.

Joe told me recently that years ago I remarked that he was a rare breed in the creative world, that he actually possessed something that most creatives lack when ideating the "Big Idea": marketing savvy. As much as I'd like to take credit for being the inspiration for this book's theme, the fact is marketing know-how is the opposite side of the same creative coin, and great work can't exist without it. And Joe was, and is, an expert on the subject!

In a cerebral way, Joe passed his creative DNA on to me and others, teaching us to have good peripheral vision of the world around us, to prevent bad things from happening to great ideas, and, ultimately, to never, ever veer toward the center and accept mediocrity.

So, if you fancy yourself the next David Ogilvy, do yourself a favor and absorb Joe's practical but so-very sage advice. Because, in the end, this is a story about how to tell a good story. Learn and enjoy!

Deb Vurpillat
VP/Director, Creative Strategy
DigitasLBi

Detroit, 2017

PREFACE

"I am a storyteller."

This is how I begin my elevator pitch.*

I continue with, "I find the people and companies that have stories to tell, I find the people who want to hear their stories, and then I create a unique, compelling and memorable way to tell those stories. Like any storyteller, my goal is to engage the audience fully and emotionally in the story so that it becomes their story too."

"Some people call it marketing communications, or advertising, or public relations or content marketing, or experiential marketing. That's what I do."

However, I started my career as a Creative, not as a marketer or consultant. I thought I was going to become a high school art teacher following my undergraduate degree. But before I could find a teaching position, I got a job as a technical illustrator. For several years I drew illustrations of auto parts and assembly processes for automotive installer manuals.

Eventually I grew frustrated with my illustrations being used ineffectively in manuals that were poorly designed. Fortunately I had the chutzpah to assert to my boss that I could design the manuals more effectively. This opportunity, along with some additional study, eventually led to a career in graphic design and art direction.

Again, I grew frustrated by concepting and designing work that didn't actually solve the clients' real problems. I was constantly asking for more information in order to do so. Instead, I was being told what to design and how to design.

I needed to understand client problems rather than simply being told how to solve them. Design and the other creative professions are problem-solving disciplines. Consequently, you have to first comprehend the real problem.

* *The premise of the elevator pitch is that you and another person get onto an elevator on the top floor of a building. You strike up a conversation. "So what do you do?" the other person asks. You have until the elevator reaches the ground floor to tell your story in such a compelling way that the other person says, "That sounds fascinating. Can I have your business card?"*

Eventually as a Creative Director, I had a client-facing role as well as an inward-facing creative role. This experience brought me closer to the clients and more able to dig deeper into the sources of client issues and problems.

Following rapid agency downsizing during a downturn in the economy, and while undertaking graduate study in Integrated Marketing Communications, I began consulting and teaching.

As a consultant I am also my own account representative. I apply what I learned during my agency jobs from the best account people with whom I had worked. I also learned what not to do, from the example of others.

My consulting specialty is informed by my understanding of the entire marketing communication process, including both the creative and account side.

For clients and agencies, I direct or improve their processes, or execute any part of the process, including analyzing and identifying problems and opportunities, devising strategy, concepting tactics, producing deliverables, evaluating results, and sourcing specialists.

The Story of this Text

The same motivation that led me to go from being a technical illustrator to a designer and creative director, and eventually to a marketing and strategy consultant, is the same motivation that led to the writing and designing of this book.

The stories in this book are true, or inspired by actual events, or combine several experiences into a single story. The names of the parties involved have been changed, although I expect that some of my former colleagues will think a particular story is about them. They will just have to guess whether or not they have correctly identified themselves.

My hope is that you, the reader, will become able to recognize the situations discussed as they arise, so as to be better able to prevent or correct problems as they occur.

Intended Audience

This book is an examination of the process and problems of communications and collaboration between the Account Team and the Creative Team in an advertising and/or marketing communications agency or company.

As such, this book is intended for educators, students and professionals, in the teaching, study, or practice of any aspect of the marketing and advertising professions.

This book can be adopted for use in courses in both account and creative disciplines, with the intention of preparing students for effective professional collaboration. Relevant courses include Account Management, Marketing, Advertising, and Business Communication, as well as in Graphic Design, Art Direction, Copywriting, Media Strategy, Content Strategy, and Creative Strategy.

This book includes exercises related to each identified problem, as well as more generally applicable exercises. While these exercises are written for a classroom setting, they are applicable to a professional setting with just a few modifications.

Additional supportive information is included to expand and augment the discussions of problems and solutions.

DEDICATION

To Marilee
my best friend
who married me

ACKNOWLEDGMENTS

My thanks for your help, guidance, expertise, and support throughout the process of the creation of this book:

Kim Bartel Sheehan, PhD, University of Oregon, who said, "You should write a book."

Stewart Gordon, PhD., historian, scholar, author, friend, advisor, and maker of cool stuff. www.stewartgordonhistorian.com,

The late Sheila Sasser, PhD., Eastern Michigan University, who was one of the most relentlessly encouraging people I have ever met.

Judy Davis, PhD., Eastern Michigan University, teacher and colleague.

The late Paul Wentzel, mentor, colleague, and friend.

Harry Briggs, publisher.

Angela Piliouras, copyeditor extraordinaire.

Debra Vurpillat, former colleague, and the person who first referred to me as a "marketing-savvy Creative."

Chapter 1

Introduction/How to Use This Book

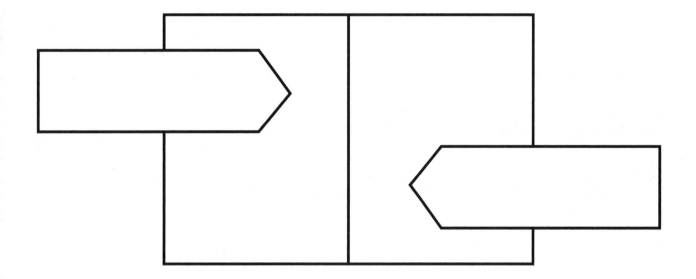

Introduction

Once upon a time (think of the Mad Men days recounted in the TV series of that name), the account guys (yes, they were all men) would bring a client opportunity to the agency. The copywriters would develop ideas, the art department would illustrate those ideas, and the creative director would approve or reject the work.

All this changed when Bill Bernbach created teams of art directors and copywriters working together under a strong strategic positioning established by the creative director.

By the time I started working, the art director/ copywriter team was a long-established, proven process.

Yet when I left the my job at the first largish agency where I had worked (for nearly a decade) for another opportunity, having given the reason that the company was going in a direction with which I did not agree, the regional president asked, "Why does some art guy care about where the business is going?"

Some "art guy"?

At that point I was the creative director with a staff of art directors, designers, and copywriters. I had rebuilt the Creative Team after a downsizing. I had developed strategic branding approaches for clients, creative business pitches that won new clients away from their incumbent agencies of record, and had gotten clients to renew long-term business.

But as far as the number one "suit" was concerned, I was just "some art guy."

While I found the reaction of the regional president disappointing, it also confirmed that I had made the right decision to leave that agency. But it was also at that same agency that a colleague referred to me as a "marketing-savvy creative."

That compliment, for I took it as such, was an important insight into what my colleagues outside the creative department actually valued in a creative collaborator. They valued a broader understanding of the challenges and objectives facing the agency as a whole, and the agency's clients in particular. While I had always sought to work in that way, I had never put a name to my own approach until then.

Those two interactions taken together, were the impetus for this book.

The contents of this book are intended to help the Account Team become "creative savvy," and the Creative Team to become "account savvy."

Working together, with greater understanding and appreciation for the challenges faced by other people, is one step toward producing more effective work.

How to Use This Book

This book has several features intended for use in your pursuit of greater understanding and improved communication between the Account and Creative Teams.

Chapter Contents
Each chapter has a contents page that not only facilitates your ability to quickly find the relevant subject in which you are interested, but also summarizes the subjects of each chapter.

Problem identification
In this book you will find a description of a typical sales process, a typical creative process, and the interface between these processes. Your particular processes may be different in terminology or more significant ways, so you should apply the ideas in this book to your own situation.

It is in the interface between these processes where the clichéd "Suits vs. Creatives" animosity manifests in negative results, rather than being a positive collaboration.

In this interface between processes, I have identified problems that frequently occur. If you have sales, agency, or freelance experience, you may recognize these problems. If you are a student with no work experience yet, you should keep these issues in mind as you begin your career, either on the creative side, on the account side, or even the client side.

I have encountered all of these problems in agency-of-record work, project-based work, and in proposal work.

Problem Stories
Throughout this book I use stories to illustrate the issues and problems I identify. All the stories are true, although some are combinations of multiple incidents, and/or have compressed time frames. Of course, I have changed the names in the stories, although I expect that some former colleagues, and actually anyone who has been in the business for some time, will recognize the characters and situations described.

Problem Explanation

Following each story you will find an explanation of the source of the problem depicted.

Solutions

One or more solutions are presented with each problem. These solutions as described are, of course, only a start. Problem solving begins with understanding, but must be accompanied by work and practice.

Problem Exercises

In addition to the solutions presented, each problem has one or more specific exercises for developing the understanding and skills needed to prevent or solve the problem.

Chapter Exercises

At the end of the problem chapters, there are longer exercises that address more than a single problem. These exercises are intended to establish useful work practices for members of both Account and Creative Teams.

Icons

You will see an icon symbolizing each of the problems identified. You can use these icons to help you recall the problems when you experience them personally.

Sidebars

You will find sidebars throughout with additional information that is relevant to the problem identified. This sidebar information may expand upon a solution or describe a useful technique for avoiding a problem.

Chapter Resources

Similarly to the end-of-chapter exercises, the chapter resources provide additional information describing useful work practices.

Chapter Notes

At the end of each chapter is a list of references for information cited within the chapter.

Glossary

Throughout the text you will find useful terms in **bold type**. These terms and their definitions can be found in the glossary.

Additional Reading

This is a list of books and articles that are related to the subjects presented herein and are useful for further reference.

Problem Icon

Problem identification

XI. The ANTI-MUSKETEER Problem

Dis-integration of the execution

Story

"The Advertising Team will present to the client first," said Dave, the advertising creative director.

"That's fine," replied Bill the account executive. "Just as long as the entire campaign works well across all media. Not like last time."

"What do you mean by that?" said Dave, accusingly.

"Well, last time, you changed the advertising at the last minute without telling the rest of the Creative Team. So that after the advertising

presentation, all the other parts of the campaign looked like they belonged to a different strategy."

"Well, that won't happen this time," said Dave. "I'll let them all know what we are doing."

"You're just letting them know now?" said Bill with dismay.

"Well, they've got all night to catch up and be ready for tomorrow," said Dave, inconsiderately.

Problem Explanation

Sometimes in the course of creative development, the ideas of each part of the Creative Team — web, print, TV and radio advertising, events, social, and PR — will start to evolve. Eventually these separate executions can come to seem as if they are very different from each other. When this happens, all of the campaign creative is not working towards the same objectives. I call this **The ANTI-MUSKETEER Problem** (not all for one anymore).

Occasionally this problem occurs because of the self-absorption of the leader of one particular team,

as in the story above. More often, though, this happens because of the inherent problem solving that occurs within each discipline. Copywriters must craft language differently for print than for web, and imagery in print differs from that on a billboard or a web banner.

This problem solving can, however, result in a difference in the look and feel, and the messaging, of individual tactical executions in different media.

This is not an intentional, willful deviation from the agreed upon creative direction. Rather, this dis-integration is the expected result of different people working on the many different parts of a complex, multi-media campaign.

Page Numbers

Chapter Number

Chapter 8

The principles of
Integrated Marketing Communications

One of the basic ideas of Integrated Marketing Communications (IMC) seems self-evident to most people when they first hear it: all the contacts a consumer has with a company or a brand should be consistent and relevant.

In practice, this means that every marketing or advertising communication from a company has a consistent message that is coordinated with all other messages.

That does not mean that all messages are identical, since the physical requirements of different media would make that impossible to achieve. For example, the words and images on a billboard that is viewed by a consumer for a few seconds as they drive by at 70 MPH, cannot be the same as the content of a catalog or product brochure that is meant to be read in detail.

Two other principles of IMC are less well known and obvious to the layperson. The first is that a company's structure must facilitate the integration of the marketing. If each product line has its own budget and marketing, the company's marketing will not be integrated.

The other principle is that each marketing tactic can be individually evaluated for effectiveness; each tactic directs a consumer to take some action, and these tactics combine in a chain to achieve the overall campaign objectives.

Sidebar

The Solution:
In order to keep the campaign truly integrated, where all creative execution across different media are complementary, although not identical, it is necessary to have regular meetings to bring the drifting executions back on track and working together.

Solution

The Disintegration Exercise:
On a team project to develop an integrated campaign, each media execution will be directed by a different person on the team.

Following the initial meeting to agree upon a creative direction, each team will only reassemble to present their individual contribution to the campaign.

Problem Exercises

Take note of how much or how little the different tactics support and coordinate with each other to create an integrated campaign.

167

Chapter 2

Suits vs. Creatives:
Who Are Those Other Guys?

*Understanding the Roles of the Creative Team
and the Account Team, and Why They Are Both Needed*

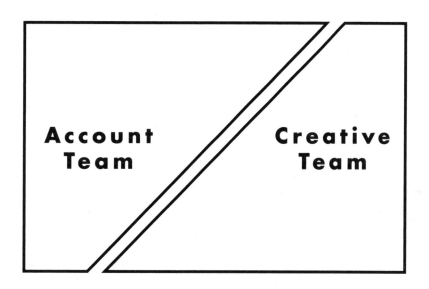

Introduction: Who Are Those Other Guys?

Understanding the roles of the Creative Team and the Account Team, and why they are both needed

The day-long mandatory training meeting began at 8 a.m. The presenter was Brad, the agency's expert and director of motivation and incentive programs. The agency created and produced a lot of sales incentive programs, which offered awards of merchandise or travel to high-performing salepersons and managers.

The incentives were usually merchandise or travel, but could also be in the form of "points" that could be redeemed for a variety of items and services. The value of the incentive was dependant on the role of the person being "incentivized."

During his morning presentation, Brad presented the premise, and philosophical underpinning, of the agency's motivation and incentive business.

Essentially, Brad contended that people only do the work they do for the extrinsic rewards they receive. People only work for pay, and

additional rewards. If a company wants their employees to perform better, rewards should be offered for improvement and achievement.

At the lunch break I approached Brad to ask a question.

"What about people who are intrinsically motivated by their passion for their work? People who are driven to do their best each day, and to exceed the previous day?"

Brad gave me a funny, quizzical look. "What is it you do for the company?" he asked.

"I'm an art director," I replied.

"Oh, you're a creative," Brad said disdainfully. "You're not like real people."

Creatives are often assumed to be "not like real people." But this assumption is based on the notion that people who have a career other than in a creative profession are the norm.

While it is true that creatives are known for approaching their work with passion, it is not true that creatives are unique in caring deeply about their work.

Brad's unspoken presumptions were that people who have not chosen a creative profession are not capable of creativity, and that the agency's "creatives" are not capable of "normality."

The reality is that many types of people are needed to make an effective agency.

In this chapter I will describe some of the types of roles within the broad categories of "Account" and "Creative."

Agency Jobs

While every advertising or marketing agency has its own version of job descriptions, responsibilities, and titles, the Advertising Educational Foundation (AEF)[1] suggests five usual categories of jobs in an advertising agency:

1. Account Management
2. Account Planning
3. Creative
4. Media
5. Interactive Marketing

For the purposes of this book, I am grouping these jobs into two divisions: the Account Team (The Suits) including Account Management and Account Planning, and the Creative Team (The Creatives) including, of course, Creative.

Media, and Interactive Marketing, as described in the AEF site, potentially have a role in both the Account Team and the Creative Team. How these roles function, and in which department they reside, depends on the specific service focus and organization of the agency, and how they define roles and responsibilities.

Other roles can include Technologist, Marketing Manager, Content Marketing Strategist, Mobile Marketing, and Social Media Strategist.

Without doubt, more roles will develop as technology and communication continue to develop. The remainder of this chapter will describe some of the roles in the Account Team and the Creative Team.

Agency Structure

There are many possible models for the structure of an agency.

While a discussion of agency organization is outside the scope of this book, it is important to recognize that the structure of the agency is relevant to processes and marketing communication integration.

For any organization, including agencies and creative services firms, the way in which the reporting and business units of the organization are structured can have a positive or negative effect.

For example, when a creative services firm groups all creatives into a pool of shared resources who may work on any account, this can positively affect the utilization of the employees. But this can also negatively impact a creative's ability to gain a deep and ongoing understanding of a specific client's business, and ultimately result in less effective work.

On the other hand, when creatives are grouped into specific account teams, the visual and written creatives can gain deep, valuable client knowledge. This comes at a higher cost to the agency, as these employees may not be fully utilized by being assigned to just one account.

Whatever the structure of the advertising agency, creative services firm, or marketing firm, the general categories of jobs described on the following pages will be included.

Introduction: Who Are Those Other Guys?

Understanding the roles of the Creative Team and the Account Team, and why they are both needed

THE SUITS, THE CREATIVES, AND EVERYONE ELSE

RESOURCES

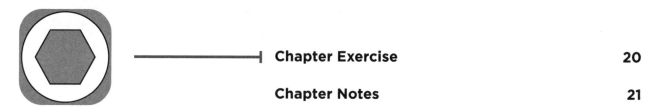

I. Account Team Roles and Responsibilities

Who are the Suits, and what do they do?

Broadly speaking, and with the understanding
that every agency is organized differently,
there are two categories of account team roles:
Account Management and **Account Planning**.

ACCOUNT MANAGEMENT
It's commonly said that the Account person is the client's voice
or representative to the agency, and is also the agency's voice
to the client.

The goal of effective **Account Management** is to facilitate solutions to clients'
problems by providing effective advertising, marketing communications,
or creative services. In addition, an Account Executive, who is typically
the leader of a Client Account Team, must accomplish this goal while also
making a profit for the agency.

Certainly part of the Account Executive's job is to develop an effective
relationship with the client, which facilitates open and productive
communication and cultivates a working partnership between the client and
the agency.

Long gone are the *Mad Men* days of "schmooze and booze," when all it took
to win a client was golf games and three-martini lunches.

Account Executives now are expected to not simply be salespersons, who
would just as likely sell shoes as advertising. Rather, they are expected to
understand effective marketing, advertising, social media, and especially to
understand the client's business as well as, or better than, the client.

As an outgrowth of the Account Executive's client knowledge, they must also
facilitate the identification of the client's real challenges and opportunities,
and be able to clearly communicate these to the Creative Team. However this
knowledge and facilitation often now falls to the Account Planner.

ACCOUNT PLANNING

Just as it's commonly said that the Account person represents the client's voice, the Account Planner represents the voice of the client's customers.

This role has also fallen to the Creative Director or the Research Department in some agencies. In other agencies, the title given to this role is "Account Creative Planner."

However, a department dedicated solely to **Account Planning** can take a longer view in planning a strategy to maintain a client's brand, or to reposition the client's brand into a more positive and unique position in the minds of consumers.

Breakthrough advertising and marketing communications is derived from relevant strategic insights into the essential motivations of a client's current and potential customers. Gleaning these insights, and developing a plan for the account, is the role of the Account Planner.

II. Creative Team Roles and Responsibilities

Who are the Creatives, and what do they do?

Broadly speaking, and with the understanding that every agency is organized differently, there have traditionally been two categories of creative team roles: Visual and Written.

Since first established by Bill Bernbach (1911-1982) in the late 1950s, the **Art Director** (Visual) and **Copywriter** (Written) team has been the basis of the Creative Team structure at advertising and creative services agencies.[2]

While this is still true at many agencies, some have expanded the Creative Team to include other disciplines as needed. I have included descriptions of these other disciplines on p. 18.

CREATIVE DEPARTMENT LEADERSHIP:

The Creative Team is headed by a **Creative Director**, who has a role that is similar to **Account Management** in that he or she is also client-facing. That is, the Creative Director must also represent the client's best interests in the agency. However, the Creative Director is also agency-facing, in that they supervise the Creative Team, and are also the Creative Team's voice to the Account Team and to the client.

The Creative Director supervises Creative Teams, and is responsible for concepting and also approving the work of the Creative Teams.

The Creative Team develops strategies and concepts, including visual communication and written communication that will connect the client with their current and potential customers.

Usually, Creative Directors previously have been Art Directors or Copywriters, but may come from the "Other" category of Creative Team disciplines (see p. 18).

The levels and titles of Creative Director, depending on the size, focus, and organization of the agency, can include Executive Creative Director, Group Creative Director, Senior Creative Director, Creative Director, and Associate Creative Director. The precise description of responsibilities will vary by title and by specific agency.

VISUAL CREATIVE

Art Directors concept and create visual communications for a variety of media. They may also direct graphic designers, illustrators, photographers, and other specialist visual creators as needed. A wide variety of executions may be used, including TV commercials, catalogs, print advertising, website and interactive, billboards, brand identity, and many others.

If you see it, an Art Director or Graphic Designer created it.

As previously mentioned, the Art Director/Copywriter team has formed the basis of the CreativeTeam since the late 1950s.

Art Directors may begin as Graphic Designers, and in many agencies the line between these disciplines has blurred over the years.

Visual Creative includes interactive and Web Designers and Web/Interactive Art Directors, though they may be in a separate Interactive Creative Department headed by an Interactive Creative Director. Visual also includes motion graphics designers, although they may be located in the Technology/Interactive or the Video and Broadcast departments, depending on the organization of the particular agency.

WRITTEN CREATIVE

Copywriters concept and create written communications across a broad range of applications for a variety of media. These include advertising copy, speech writing, technical writing, direct marketing copy, catalog copy, video and motion scripting and dialogue, press releases, and many others. A Copywriter may also develop content and write for social media.

Each of these types of writing is a specialty, although a Copywriter is usually skilled at multiple applications and styles of writing.

III. Other Roles and Responsibilities

Who are they, and what do they do?

In addition to the Account Team and Creative Team roles described, agencies have added essential new roles as marketing communications and technology have changed.

MEDIA

The **Media Department** in an agency researches, plans, and contracts with a media company to place the advertising and marketing communications where the intended target audience will be most likely to see, interact with, and remember it. Options go beyond broadcast television and print advertising in magazines and newspapers, which were the traditional media for advertising. Media now includes cable television, internet advertising, on demand and streaming television and video, before-movie ads, and mobile device ad placement.

This "placement" of advertising is an integral part of the effectiveness of the campaign, and must also be done in a cost-effective way.

For a long time, advertising placement commissions were a major source of the agency's revenue. That is no longer usually true, and media agencies responsible for only the media planning and placement are often separate entities from the advertising agency.

TECHNOLOGY/INTERACTIVE

Interactive Art Directors and Interactive Copywriters may be located in the Interactive Creative Department. They will also work together to concept and create visual and written communications and advertising.

Web developers, app developers, engineers, creative coders, and other technologists are often located in the Information Technology (IT) Department, but may have Creative Team roles on specific projects.

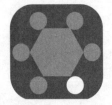

RESEARCH, CONSUMER BEHAVIOR, ANALYTICS

These related functions study and describe what consumers think, feel, and do. Gaining the understanding of how people make decisions, how they behave, and what actions they take is the source of meaningful insights that guide the creation of effective marketing communications and advertising, and can help prove that the campaigns have been successful. Analytics are also used during a campaign to identify underperforming tactics so that improvements can be made, or budgets reallocated to more successful efforts.

SOCIAL MEDIA

The **Social Media Manager** develops strategy, plans and develops content, manages content placement on relevant social media channels, and monitors the effectiveness of those choices.

The Social Media Manager's objective is often to develop fans and followers, and then to help turn those fans into customers.

A Social Media Manager will also moderate and respond to public comments in an effort to turn doubters into advocates, and to foster deeper audience engagement with a brand.

Social Media Managers have a significant role participating in, or interacting with, the Creative Team.

VIDEO AND BROADCAST

Video and Broadcast Producers manage all aspects of pre-production, production and post-production of video for placement on a variety of media. This includes sourcing on-screen talent, scouting locations or booking studio space, shooting, recording, and editing.

Producers work closely with the Creative Team that develops the concepts, visuals, storyboards, and copy that inform the video production.

AGENCY MANAGEMENT AND AGENCY SUPPORT

The people managing the agency, and the people providing the administrative support, are essential to profitable operations.

More than that, management establishes and maintains the agency's brand and the work environment for everyone there.

The administrative support people are essential to the smooth operation of the agency, and are often the key people to know in order to get things done in a timely and efficient way.

Chapter Exercise

Developing a Plan to Become Qualified for the Job You Want

1. Research careers in Advertising, Marketing, Creative, and Public Relations at the online organization for those disciplines. Here are a few to get you started.

    • The Advertising Education Foundation. www.aef.com
    • American Association of Advertising Agencies. www.aaaa.org
    • The American Marketing Association. www.ama.org
    • American Institute of Graphic Arts. www.aiga.org

2. Pick those disciplines that interest you for further research.

3. Look up entry level job postings on online job boards such as Monster. com, Indeed.com, Careerbuilder.com, and others, for each of the disciplines that interests you. Read those job listings and take note of the qualifications for those jobs.

4. Make a list of the required skills and knowledge described in the posted jobs.

5. Find courses and books from which you can gain the knowledge and skills to develop the qualifications required for those jobs.

6. Develop a plan, including a timeline, to take those courses, read those books, create a portfolio (if required), and write your resume.

Chapter Notes

1. Advertising Career Possibilities. (2009). Retrieved from www.aef.com/industry/careers/9000
2. William Bernbach. (1999). Retrieved from www.adage.com/article/special-report-the-advertising-century/william-bernbach/140180/

Chapter 3

What's Wrong With Those Other Guys?

The Causes of the Divide Between the Creative Team and the Account Team; or Why is it Suits vs. Creatives?

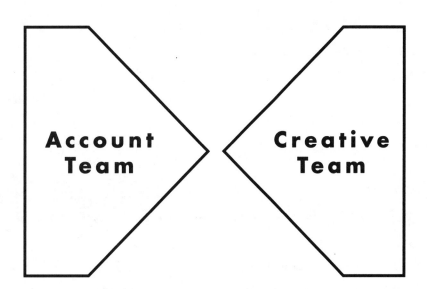

Introduction: What's Wrong with Those Other Guys?

The Causes of the Divide Between the Creative Team and the Account Team; or Why is it Suits vs. Creatives?

"We should meet to discuss this opportunity," said Lester wearily at the end of the day. Lester was my boss, and owner of the small agency where I got my first art direction job.

"Absolutely," I replied enthusiastically. *"How about now? Or late tomorrow morning? Or tomorrow afternoon?"*

"I'm busy all afternoon," said Lester. *"I'll schedule a meeting for tomorrow morning at seven."*

"Um...," I began. *"I can certainly be here. But,"* I continued, *"I'm going to be here late working on this project. And I know we've talked about this before, but I really am not at my best that early in the day."*

"I know you've said that before," replied Lester. *"But that's all in your state of mind, and..."*

"Actually, it's not," I countered. *"There are several studies showing..."*

"...After all," continued Lester, oblivious to my objections, *"I am in here early every day. I listen to motivational tapes on the drive in too!"*

"Yes, and thanks for the copy of the tape you wanted us all to listen to," I said. *"But by 2:30 in the afternoon you're toast, while I gain energy throughout the day."*

"I do get tired as the day goes on," Lester admitted. *"But that's the right way to do it!"*

"OK," I sighed. *"I'll see you here tomorrow morning at seven."*

"See you then," said Lester, as he walked out the door to go home, while I returned to my desk to continue working.

The notion of "Suits versus Creatives" has been something of an accepted fact in the agency world.

Why is this so? What is the source of this problem, this divide?

As this story illustrates, people have preferred ways of working. Not everyone understands nor accepts that.

My boss believed that everyone should approach their work as he did. But as I tried on many occasions to explain, a different way of working doesn't mean a wrong way.

This is true not only of morning "larks" versus "night owls."*

The Account Team and the Creatives often approach their work with a different focus.

They use different **Jargon**. Consequently, the same words can have different meanings.

Because of their focus, each team follows a different process.

Improving understanding has the potential to combat this traditional animosity, and to reduce the biggest underlying problem of "**Othering**" — a concept that refers to thinking about "those other guys" as being wrong simply because of what they do differently.

* *I was correct when I said to my boss that there is a spectrum of morning-to-evening persons, who are referred to as "larks" and "night owls." Look in the Chapter Notes for an article about this subject.[1]*

Introduction: What's Wrong with Those Other Guys?

The Causes of the Divide Between the Creative Team and the Account Team; or Why is it Suits vs. Creatives?

THE DIFFERENCES BETWEEN SUITS AND CREATIVES

RESOURCES

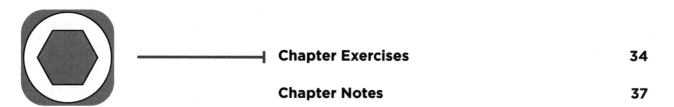

I. DIFFERENT FOCUS

Marketing and sales, marketing and brand building, and
what motivates the Account Team and the Creative Team

The Account Team Focus
In very general terms, the Account Team is focused on either, or ideally
both, short-term marketing and sales, and long-term marketing, customer
relationships, and brand building.

The short-term focus is often a component of job descriptions for "Marketing
and Sales Representatives." Short-term marketing is often thought to be
about generating sales and revenue. By contrast, long-term marketing is
thought to be about establishing and maintaining the brand to capture
market share and develop loyal customers.

Both types of marketing are needed, since a company won't survive long
enough to develop a successful brand without the revenue and profitability
to continue in business. However, the long-term brand value of a company
can be damaged by a singular focus on gaining short-term revenue in a way
that erodes consumer confidence and trust.

The Creative Team Focus

The Creative Team is focused on either, or ideally both, the conceptual and strategic, or the practical and tactical.*

Some projects and campaigns require a conceptual and strategic approach to develop a brand's long-term viability and success, as in the approach taken by the marketing and brand building Account Team mentioned above.

Other projects require a practical approach to marketing communications tactics in order to drive the shorter-term sales and revenue, as also mentioned above.

The apparent difference in focus of the Account and Creative Teams is when one team is focused on a short-term solution, while the other is focused on a long-term solution.

This mismatch can be addressed when the Account Team and the Creative Team understand their joint focus, and take a client- and solution-oriented approach to their work.

* *"Tactical" in this sense does not mean dressed in black or camouflage print, straps and buckles, and carrying MOLLE-compatible equipment. Tactical refers to tactics, such as advertising, direct marketing, or other specific means of marketing communication.*

II. DIFFERENT JARGON

What they say, and what they mean

Why Jargon?

Every group, society, profession, and organization has its own unique terminology. Such jargon serves not only to facilitate communication within the group by abbreviating longer explanations, but also allows the members of the group to easily recognize each other.

During a job interview, it is common for the interviewer to ask questions using job-specific jargon, and to expect the interviewee to answer using jargon correctly.

Jargon is closely related to buzzwords and buzz phrases, such as the clichéd "let's run it up the flagpole and see if anyone salutes." Jargon, however, is terminology that has exact, specialized meaning within a profession.

A problem arises when the Account Team and the Creative Team use different terms not generally understood by the other team, or use the same term to mean different things.

The solution, for both the Account Team and the Creative Team, is to learn more about the practices, processes, and terminology of the other disciplines, and when confronted with an unfamiliar term, to ask questions.

Shared Jargon Used Differently

While jargon specific to Account and Marketing, and Creative are too extensive to completely cover here, one of the most frequently used and important terms used by both teams is **Key Performance Indicator (KPI).**

Because there are many types of KPIs, this is a term often used by both the Account and Creative Teams, which can lead to confusion. While the best agencies understand and manage these differences, in general the Account Team KPIs are focused on sales and profitability (see ROI on the following page), while the Creative Team KPIs are focused on the effective use of time and the project results.

The Creative KPIs can include how much time a project actually took the Creative Team to accomplish (Actual Project Time) compared to the estimate of time before the work was begun (Estimated Project Time). The time estimate is essential to establishing a budget for the creative work to be done if the agency is using a method referred to as **Cost-Plus Pricing**.

This method sets a billable rate per hour of work by agency employees, multiplies this rate times the hours required to accomplish a given task, then adds a percentage for profit.

No matter the fee structure of the agency, however, accurate estimates of time required are an essential element contributing to profitability.

Agency management will also have KPIs for the performance of the entire agency as a business organization, including billable versus non-billable time reported by staff; staff utilization (how much billable time are agency employees reporting); and under-, on-, and over-budget client projects.

Some Account Team Jargon

The Account Team focus, as discussed on previous pages, gives rise to specific jargon especially related to sales and profitability. Two of the most important terms are Return on Investment (ROI) and **Return on Marketing Investment (ROMI)**. See "How to Calculate Return on Marketing Investment" on p. 159 for more information.

ROMI has both a short-term, tactical formula for calculating the effect of a specific communications effort, and a longer-term, campaign-relevant formula.

One of the challenges of calculating ROMI is **attribution**, another term of jargon. Attribution refers to determining which piece of communication had the effect of moving a specific consumer to take action. A related problem is understanding what contribution each **impression** (referring to one person's exposure to an example of advertising on one occasion) had to the overall success of the effort.

Some Creative Team Jargon

Creative Team professionals develop their own jargon. Some examples include design-specific terms, such as the **Principles of Design** (see p. 81) that are relevant in the Creative Process (see Chapter 5). Also commonly used are **FPO (For Position Only),** referring to a placeholder image that will not be used in the final work, and **Greeking**, referring to placeholder text composed of nonsense words or Latin, that show the correct typeface usage but not the final wording. Just like Account Team jargon, there is too much Creative jargon to completely cover here.

Copywriters also have specific jargon, depending on the type of writing. A few limited examples of these terms are **voice** (a distinct brand personality expressed in words), **lede** (the introductory part of the story), and **inverted pyramid** (a structure for prioritizing and presenting information).

The Creative Team has many other specific terms of art. See The Jargon Problem, p. 152.

III. DIFFERENT PROCESSES

How each team goes about their work

When I was beginning my career, I was advised always to have a pencil in my hand and paper in front of me when I was thinking. In that way an Account Team person walking by my desk would think I was working rather than simply daydreaming.

This illustrates the potential for misunderstanding between the Account and Creative Teams because they follow different processes. The Creatives are not always "daydreaming," on social media, or playing games. The Account Team is not always on the golf course or at the legendary "three-martini lunch"* entertaining a client.

By necessity, the processes employed by the Account and Creative Teams are different. In Chapter 4, The Account Team Process, and Chapter 5, The Creative Team Process, I describe general processes for each team. The specifics of these process will vary at different agencies.

In Chapter 6, The Road to Successful Collaboration, I describe one model for a workflow between the Account and Creative Teams. This workflow process will also vary by agency. Many agencies continue to experiment with different processes to adapt to new media and technologies, improve the integration of the disciplines, and to improve results for their clients.

It is important for both the Account and Creative Teams, as well as the Agency Management, to understand the processes of the teams. This is a necessary step to ensure accountability within the disciplines, as well as to minimize misunderstandings between the teams.

> *I had always found the idea of a three-martini lunch confusing, since three martinis would mean a nap and a possible hangover for me rather than a return to the office. However, when my wife and I visited the legendary Harry's New York Bar on the Rue Daunou in Paris,[2] I learned how this might have been feasible.
>
> Monsieur Gérard, the master bartender, dressed in a white lab coat with his name embroidered on the upper left pocket, took our orders: a gin martini for Marilee, and a dirty vodka martini for me. We watched Gerard's mastery of mixology as he created our drinks. He served them to us in the smallest martini glasses we had ever seen.
>
> These glasses were the actual traditional size for a martini glass, and are about one-third the size of the martini glasses currently used by many bars and restaurants.
>
> Consequently, a three-martini lunch in the days of Alex Osborn (see p. 80) and Bill Bernbach could be the equivalent of a single martini today.

IV. OTHERING

Getting along with people who are different

"Those guys"
"Suits"
"Some art guy"
"Code monkey"
"Schmoozer"
"Word jockey"

Othering

One significant impediment to improved communication and collaboration between the Account and Creative Teams is explained by "**othering**," which refers to treating a person or group of people as different, alien, or not one of "us." They are the "others."

Both as a cause and consequence, the other group may be viewed as of less importance or value. Some employees may begin to practice othering as a means of fitting into their agency's culture. This can be a continuation of what students experience if they were pigeonholed as nerds, jocks, and others during school. Remember the movie "The Breakfast Club?"

While othering is most frequently used to describe how bigotry based on race, gender and gender expression, sexual orientation, religion, disability, and other perceived differences arises and is practiced, the concept of **Othering** also describes how some teams treat those of other disciplines, even within the same agency.

Microaggressions

Microaggressions are a result of, and a way to recognize, the practice of othering. "The term racial microaggressions, was first coined by psychiatrist Chester Pierce, MD, in the 1970s. But the concept is also rooted in the work of Jack Dovidio, Ph.D. (Yale University) and Samuel Gaertner, Ph.D. (University of Delaware)."[3]

Microaggressions "are the brief and everyday slights, insults, indignities and denigrating messages" directed at members of one group by a person of another group. The term microaggressions, just as the term Othering, is most frequently used as the cited author does, to refer to such messages directed at a person of a different race.[4]

Applying these terms describing dysfunctional, bigoted interactions to groups within an agency could be seen as the trivialization of a critically important social issue. However, it is my sincere hope that by applying the understanding of these concepts to the interactions between people in an agency setting, we can recognize such behaviors, and thereby begin to learn to function together more equitably.

Chapter Exercises

Exercise 1: Picking a Focus (Objective)

The purpose of this exercise is to improve your understanding of, and ability to define, a clear focus and objective for a project.

This exercise can be done as a class, with discussion.

1. Pick an assignment from one of your classes; it doesn't need to be an advertising class. Some assignments have a clear statement of the reason for the assignment, while in other assignments the purpose is implied.

2. If your assignment has a clear statement of purpose, extract that statement from the assignment instructions.

    2.a. Write a different purpose or objective for the assignment, then answer these questions:
    1. How do you need to change your approach based on the different focus? What different or additional steps are needed to accomplish the new assignment?
    2. Is additional research required to accomplish the new version of the assignment?

3. If your assignment's purpose is implied, write a clear statement of the purpose of the assignment.

    3. a. Compare your statements of purpose to those of other students. How are your statements similar or different? Why? What led you to your conclusion?

Exercise 2: Developing a Process

The purpose of this exercise is to expand on the part of Exercise 1 that asks you to revise your approach based on a new focus.

This exercise can be done on the board as a class collaboration.

1. Choose the current assignment objective or your new objective.
2. Draw a process diagram on a whiteboard or flip chart page, illustrating the process steps. Keep the diagram simple.

For example:

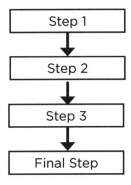

This is a basic model, so you should add more steps and as much detail as needed.

3. Now consider how you would change or add steps when working with a group. What steps could be done by different people working at the same time? Then add a coordination meeting as a step, to make certain that the work done individually can be seamlessly integrated with the other parts.

For example:

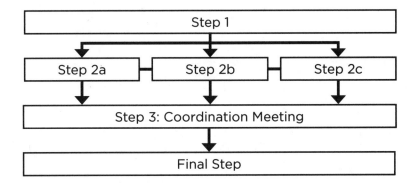

Chapter Exercises

Exercise 3: Identifying Your Own Jargon

The purpose of this exercise is to illuminate how much jargon you are already using in your group participation. This exercise can be done as a group in class, or individually.

1. List the groups and organizations of which you have been a member.
2. Pick one of the organizations. If working on this exercise as a team, pick a group in which several of you have participated.
3. Write down as many unique terms (jargon) specific to that organization. The terms can be particular words and acronyms, or can be a common word with a meaning specific to that organization.
4. As a group, present these terms to the class, one at a time, without explanation.
5. As you present each term, members of the class should suggest definitions for the terms you present.
6. Once all suggestions are given, you should tell the class the correct meaning of the term, and if possible the origin of that term.

Chapter Notes

1. Jaffe, Eric. (2015). "Morning People Vs. Night Owls: 9 Insights Backed By Science." Retrieved from www.fastcodesign.com/3046391/evidence/morning-people-vs-night-people-9-insights-backed-by-science
2. Harry's New York Bar, Paris. (2016). Retrieved from http://harrysbar.fr/en/
3. Sue, Derald Wing. (2010). "Racial Microaggressions in Everyday Life." Retrieved from www.psychologytoday.com/blog/microaggressions-in-everyday-life/201010/racial-microaggressions-in-everyday-life
4. Ibid.

Chapter 4

How Advertising and Marketing Communications Are Sold

The Account Team Process; or
How the Suits Sell the Stuff the Creatives Make

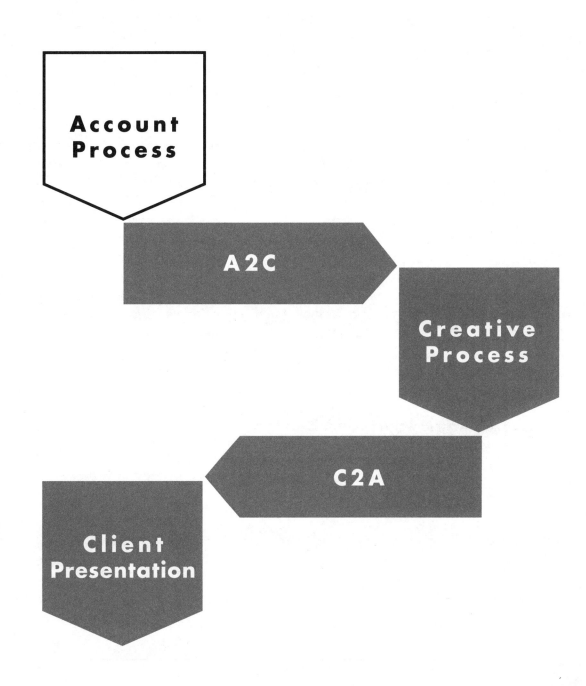

Introduction: How Advertising and Marketing Communications Are Sold

The Account Team process; or how the Suits sell the stuff the Creatives make

"How's it going?" I asked Sue the account project manager, as she came into the mat room where I was assembling materials for the upcoming client presentation.

"Well..." Sue began.

"What's up?" I sighed.

"They're discussing the background color of the presentation," said Sue.

"The top global executives of this agency are assembled in our conference room on the eve of a presentation for a very large and important account, and they are screwing around talking about the color of the background?" I asked, incredulously.

"Yes," replied Sue. "They've been at it for almost 30 minutes."

"You might want to watch this," I said, as I headed for the conference room.

I quietly let myself into the room. I listened for two minutes as the discussion about the background color continued.

"Excuse me," I said to the room, as I stood.

"I know that on the eve of this presentation you all have important decisions to make regarding many critical issues of our proposal."

"Tell ya what," I continued. "I'll take care of the background color of the presentation so that you don't have to worry about it. Then you can instead focus on the important issues."

With that, I turned and left the room, with absolute certainty that we had already lost the new account.

The Account Team necessarily is concerned with both selling the agency's services, and for improving their existing clients' sales.

The account and marketing process ideally is focused on the client's business needs by:

1. Analyzing the opportunity in the marketplace, discovering unmet needs, and determining what the potential is for viable success; then
2. Analyzing the competition. Who are they, what is their market share, who are their customers? What are they currently doing to reach their customers?

These analyses lead to setting objectives, which can be, for example, an increase in market share, an increase in sales, or retaining customers. There are many ways to define success.

The paradox is that if the Account Team is focused on making the sale, rather than on solving the client's business problem, then the Account Team often will accomplish neither.

Introduction: How Advertising and Marketing Communications Are Sold

The Account Team process; or how the Suits sell the stuff the Creatives make

THE ACCOUNT TEAM PROCESS

I. IDENTIFY and/or CREATE the Opportunity

How the Account Team identifies opportunities

Business Development and Lead Generation

Lead generation is the process of stimulating interest among relevant audiences for the purpose of developing possible sales opportunities.

While new business development can be undertaken on behalf of a client as part of an agency's services, as described here this step refers to developing new business for the agency itself.

Just as for a client, this step is essential to develop interest among potential clients in the agency's brand and services. This task may be undertaken by either the agency's Account Team, business development team, or marketing team.

The identification of opportunities requires research, contacting prospective clients, and conducting analysis of those potential clients and their business sectors. Eventually, new opportunities can be the result of the Account Team developing an ongoing relationship with a client. Such a relationship can ideally lead to the agency being included on **requests for proposal (RFPs)**, and requests to bid on **agency-of-record** business.

This step of the account process is sometimes referred to as "filling the funnel," referring to the opening of a traditional **purchase funnel** (see pp. 52–53 for a discussion of this and newer models of consumer attitudes and purchase behavior).

B2B Not B2C

The process of developing a new account for an agency is more akin to the **Business-to-Business (B2B)** process than it is to the **Business-to-Consumer (B2C)** process.

While an agency may use many of the B2C lead generation techniques available, since the focus of an agency is on improving their clients' businesses, this is a B2B sales effort.

B2B lead generation techniques in common with B2C include **search engine optimization (SEO)** and **paid search**.

Agencies will also use highly targeted **direct marketing,** trade shows, conferences, **webinars**, and other **content marketing** to engender new business opportunities.

Content as a Lead Generation Technique
The Content Marketing Institute defines their discipline as "the strategic marketing approach [that] focuses on creating and distributing valuable, relevant, and consistent content to attract and retain a clearly-defined audience — and, ultimately, to drive profitable customer interaction."[1]

In a B2B context, engaging and relevant content will help to position the agency as the "go to" thought and practice leaders in a particular area of expertise. This drives potential clients to seek out the agency for help, rather than the agency always and only looking for new client opportunities.

Although some content marketers define everything as "content," some specific examples include blogs, white papers, eBooks, webinars, infographics, speeches, and events.

Content must be specifically planned as part of the agency's overall strategic approach to branding and new business development.

II. ANALYZE and QUALIFY the Opportunity

How the Account Team determines that the opportunity
is worth pursuing

The Go or No Go Decision

When an agency Account Team has received a **Request for Proposal (RFP)**,
the agency must determine whether to submit a proposal or decline the
invitation to submit a bid.

The decision to respond with a proposal (the Go Decision) will be based on
the assessment of the Account Team and the agency management about the
potential profitability of the business. While other factors may be considered,
such as whether this piece of business will lead to other business with the
agency or in that business sector, many agencies have undertaken money-
losing accounts with the hope that other, more profitable business will result.
That anticipated, hoped-for business usually does not materialize, so this
likelihood must also be considered.

It is important to recognize that developing a response to an RFP takes
time and agency personnel to research, write, budget, proofread, and
otherwise prepare. Additionally, for a full response, the Creative Team
will become involved in concepting, writing, and visualizing the proposed
creative approach.

This agency response costs the agency money. If the agency doesn't win the
account, then this cost represents a loss to the agency. If the agency wins the
account, the costs of developing the response will be included in the overall
project budget.

Types of Responses to RFP

- **Decline**
  When the decision is "No Go" the agency replies with a courteously
  worded professional letter thanking the client, but stating that they
  decline to submit a proposal for this opportunity.
- **Standardized response**
  Sometimes the agency will respond with a standardized document,
  outlining the agency's capabilities and a proposed budget. Often referred
  to as "boiler plate" copy, this standardized document is a starting point,
  and is customized to the specific client, then proofread for accuracy and
  appropriateness. Submitting a rework of a previous RFP response that
  still includes a different client's name* is a certain way of guaranteeing
  that the agency will lose the bid.

* I've actually seen this happen. We did not win that account.

- **White paper**

  This response includes strategy, staff profiles, examples of previous work, and budget. Often called a **white paper** because this response is a text-only document with limited formatting and no graphics. While this type of response may include "boiler plate" copy, more content and client specifics are included than in the standardized response.

- **Full response**

  This response includes strategy, staff profiles, proposed creative approach, including sample executions (designs, ads, storyboards, animatics, website, and other "**comps**"), and budget. This **"spec work"** is thought to increase the likelihood of winning the account, or may be required by the client.

What is "Spec Work"?

A full response to an RFP includes the proposed creative approach. Since this creative work is not being paid for by a client, it is being undertaken on a purely speculative basis, and is therefore referred to as "spec work."

Spec work poses a risk for the agency, because it takes the same effort and follows the same creative process as developing paid work. This costs the agency time, effort, and ultimately, money for an account they may not win. Agencies hate doing spec work.

When to Decline the Invitation to Bid

When the Account Team and agency management conclude that no substantially profitable opportunity exists, and there is no other compelling reason to try to win the account, the agency will respond by declining the opportunity to submit a proposal. Another reason to decline, or to submit a minimal response, is when the agency determines that they are only a "**check bid**."

What is a "Check Bid"?

Often a company will have in place a bidding process that requires a certain minimum number of agencies to bid on the work. When there is an incumbent agency who is virtually guaranteed to win the account, then the other agencies are only bidding for the purpose of fulfilling the "number of bidders" requirement of the company. Essentially, the agency is enabling the company to "check" that number requirement off their list.

III. ANALYZE the Marketplace

How the Account Team understands the client and the competition

Analyzing and understanding the market environment of a client is an essential business function. This analysis enables an understanding about the client's marketplace position, strengths, and weaknesses, and those of their competition.

Marketplace Analysis

One form of summarizing this information is the **SWOT Analysis**. In this analysis, the Strengths, Weaknesses, Opportunities, and Threats in the marketplace are described; this is elaborated upon in greater detail following this summary SWOT table:

	Positive	Negative
Internal	**Strengths** • • •	**Weaknesses** • • •
External	**Opportunities** • • •	**Threats** • • •

As you can see by the table, the Strengths (positive) and Weaknesses (negative) are Internal to the client company, while the Opportunities (positive) and Threats (negative) are External.

This analysis may be done by the Account Team, the business intelligence team, or the marketing research team, depending on the organization of a particular agency.

Competitive Analysis

The analysis can be framed by answering these important questions:

Who is the client's competition and what is the competition doing?

An understanding of the client's competition results in information the Creative Team requires to craft and effective solution.

In addition to information about the competition's financial position and market share, the Creative Team will want samples of the competition's marketing communications. These samples, and samples of the client's previous communications, help the Creative Team to craft solutions that position the client advantageously.

Providing such information and samples will contribute to, or minimize the efforts required during the Creative Team Process (Step C2, Research Focus: Client Communication Audit and Competitive Communication Audit, pp. 68-69).

How well is the competition succeeding?

This expands upon the External Threat section of the SWOT. Details about the competition's efforts and success or failures informs the Creative Team's solution development.

Since a Creative solution needs to be effective and original, the Creative Team must avoid the look and messaging of previously used marketing communications by the client or their competition. However, previous successes and failures inform the development of an effective solution by providing the team the opportunity to glean insights into important audience motivations.

Gaining such insights into audience motivations is one objective of the next step in the Account Team Process (Step A4, pp. 50-51).

IV. ANALYZE the Audience

How the Account Team understands a client's current
and potential customers

Analyzing the current and potential customers of a client is an essential business function. This analysis enables an understanding not only of the descriptive particulars of the current and potential customers of a client, but seeks to understand the essential motivations of these customers.

This analysis may be done by the account team, the business intelligence team, or the marketing research team, depending on the organization of a particular agency.

Demographics, Psychographics, and More

The relevant attributes of potential customers of a company fall within the categories of **demographics** and **geographics**. These attributes include age, gender, marital status, educational status, household income, and location.

The mental attributes of these customers are referred to as **psychographics**. This refers to their attitudes, interests, activities, opinions, and aspirations.

Correlating the demographic and psychographic information about current and potential customers leads to accurately segmenting the potential audience for the client, in order to more precisely target the relevant consumer groups.

Consumer Segmentation

Demographic descriptions of age groups, such as Baby Boomers or Millennials, are broad categorizations. However, it is necessary to understand the psychographic differences between sub-segments of a particular group.

For example, the younger Millennials may still be in college, or have recently graduated, while the older Millennials may be employed, married, and have children. Therefore the needs of these sub-segments are different, and the solutions directed at these groups will be different as well.

Therefore, it is far less likely that an automotive company will market minivans to younger, single Millennials, but instead will target older Millennials and other groups with spouses and small children.

Similarly, the aspirations, attitudes, and needs of people living in large cities may be different from those of people living in smaller cities and rural areas.

Using the automotive company example again, it is far less likely that a full-sized, powerful pickup truck will be marketed to people living in large cities where parking is expensive, public transportation is available, and the utility of a pickup is not needed for regular tasks. In New York City, 55.7 % of households do not own a vehicle, while in Scranton, Pennsylvania only 16.2% of households do not own a vehicle.[2]

Although this example refers to all households in those cities, this begins to show that specific sub-segmentation can lead to insights that inform the marketing and advertising solutions.

V. DEFINE SUCCESS

How the Account Team will prove return on investment

In order to demonstrate to a client that the agency's efforts were successful, the Account Team and the client must agree on the definition of success for a particular project or campaign.

Sometimes a client will simply say "sell more" as a definition of success. However, increased sales is not always the goal of a campaign.

Depending on the client company's position in the marketplace, the goal may include increasing the company's presence in a particular market segment, or expanding into a new geographic market, or increasing profits (which is not the same thing as selling more).

In the marketplace, a company that is new and largely unknown may focus on making consumers aware of their products or services. A company that is established and successful with a particular consumer sub-segment may want to offer additional products or services to that sub-segment, or reach a new sub-segment. A company that is well established but is losing market share will wish to recapture lost customers and find new ones. A company that is no longer the market leader and is in need of revitalization may wish to introduce new products or services, relaunch and redefine their brand, or find new audiences for their products or services.

Referring to the now-outdated traditional purchase funnel model (figure 1), an account team may want to enlarge the audience of potential customers (widen the top of the funnel, figure 2), or shorten the time from the beginning of the process until consumers make purchases and become loyal customers (shorten the height of the funnel, figure 3), or they may want to convert more of consumers into customers who will make purchases (straighten the sides of the funnel, figure 4).

See also the sidebar "Specific Tactics and the ~~Purchase~~ **Brand Attitude Funnel**," on p. 107. (The word Purchase is intentionally crossed out above to indicate that the model is no longer adequately descriptive of consumer purchasing behavior. The model is still useful as a starting point for gaining an understanding of some objectives of the Account Team, and for understanding the relationship of marketing communication tactics to achieving specific objectives.)

The final step of the Account Team process takes these client goals and expands them into specific program objectives.

On the following page is an updated model of a consumer decision/purchasing/brand attitude map (figure 5). While the same objectives of increasing the audience, retaining audience by engagement throughout the process, and building loyal customers remain, the consumer path is more varied and complex.

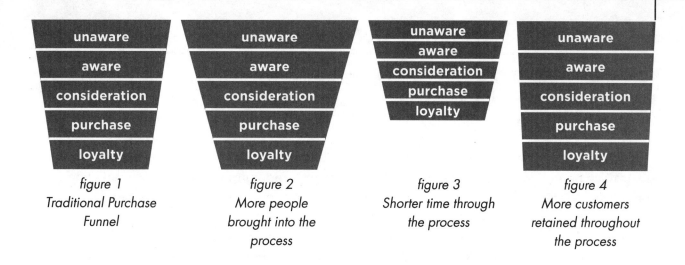

figure 1
Traditional Purchase
Funnel

figure 2
More people
brought into the
process

figure 3
Shorter time through
the process

figure 4
More customers
retained throughout
the process

figure 5
Updated consumer decision/purchasing/brand attitude map

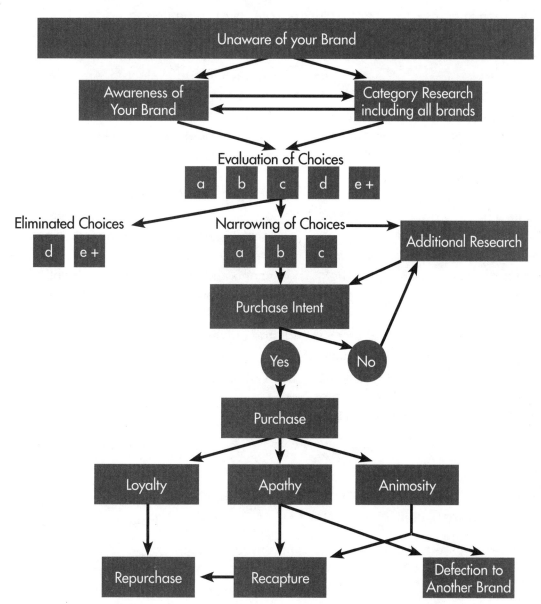

VI. DEFINE THE PRIMARY OBJECTIVES

How the Account Team determines what the agency
needs to accomplish for the client

Finally, after steps 1 through 5, and once the goals have been defined (see Step A5, p. 52) the **primary objectives** must be defined. These are the objectives of the overall campaign or program, rather than the **tactical objectives**, which are the goals for each specific marketing communications effort. It is essential that these primary objectives be accurately defined in terms of the actual problems that a client faces, rather than in terms of a tactical solution that will not address the real situation. (See **The TAKING THE WRONG PRESCRIPTION Problem**, p. 148).

To be effective, a primary objective must be defined in terms of the specific audience demographically and geographically, the quantified result, and the time frame.

For example, a primary objective could be "in 12 months *(time frame)* increase sales to older Millennials with families *(specific targeted audience)* by 20% *(quantified result)* over the previous calendar year."

However, such an objective will not be achieved simply by a one-step, direct process of simply asking people to buy more. Rather, primary objectives are achieved through the success of connected chains of tactics, each with its own **tactical objective.**

These connected tactics can include outgoing marketing communications, such as direct marketing or advertising, or incoming traffic to the company's website.

Incoming traffic can come from a search engine, requiring search engine marketing and optimization, or through social media.

Outgoing marketing communications may also direct consumer traffic to the same websites as does a consumer initiated search. That is why tracking codes and other source identification methods should be used on outgoing communications.

In this way, the effectiveness of each tactic can be tracked and evaluated. An underperforming tactic can break the chain of connected tactics. Poorly performing tactics should be eliminated so the budget can be reallocated to other, more effective tactics.

The tactics work together to achieve the primary, overall objectives. **Tactical Integration Mapping**, described on the following page, is a method of graphically describing these connected chains, in order to identify measurable links, and understand how the success of each tactic contributes to achieving the primary objectives.

Tactical Integration Mapping

This is a technique of graphically visualizing the interactions of marketing communications campaign components.

The purpose of Tactical Integration Mapping is to identify opportunities for consumer engagement, campaign integration, gaps in measurement, or additional "calls to action" for individual communications.

For a description of the Tactical Integration Mapping process, see Exercise 2 on pp. 58-59.

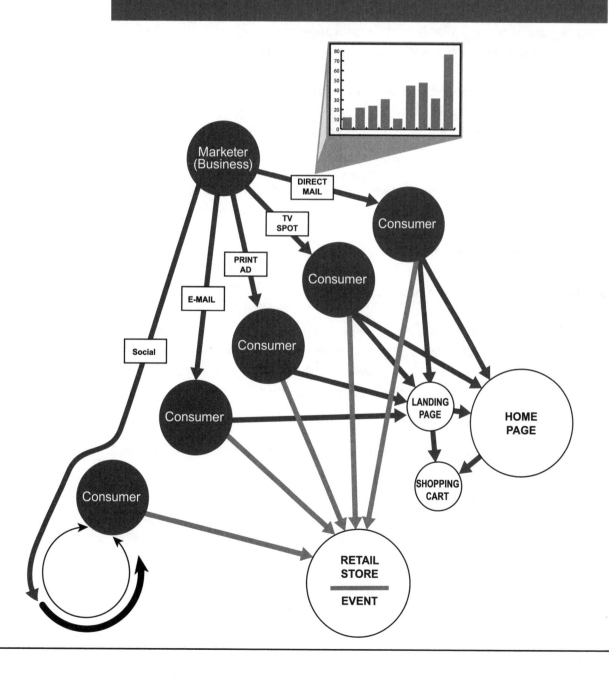

Chapter Exercises

Exercise 1: Role Switching

At most universities, the design and writing programs are offered in the College of Arts and Sciences, while the marketing, advertising, and business programs are offered in the College of Business.

Because of this separation, few students get the opportunity to collaborate with people studying the other disciplines.

The purpose of this exercise is to give the students of each discipline the opportunity to gain understanding by practicing the other role.

This exercise can be conducted over a period of weeks.

1. If you are a design or writing student, you will participate as a member of an Account Team.

   If you are a marketing, advertising, or business student, you will participate in a Creative Team, either as Copywriter or an Art Director.

   A group of students will take the role of a Client Team.

Students assuming the role of a Client Team:

2. The Client Team will research a real company, so that real data and secondary research is available for this exercise. This part of the exercise should be divided between the members of the team, and be done outside of class. Suggested duration of this part of the exercise is one to two weeks.

3. Based on their research, the Client Team will meet to develop objectives for the other teams to accomplish.

Students assuming the role of the Account Team:

4. The Account Team will interview the Client Team. Their goal is to follow the account process in order to determine the "client's" objectives. This step of the exercise could occur during a class meeting.

5. The Account Team should then research the marketplace and competition, and write a SWOT analysis. The Account Team will then present this analysis to the Creative Team and the class. Suggested duration of this part of the exercise is one to two weeks.

Students assuming the role of the Creative Team:

6. The Creative Team will meet to develop a strategy, including branding and positioning, and specify tactics (without designing or writing any executions of these tactics) needed to accomplish the objectives (see The Difference Between Marketing and Creative Strategies, p. 103).

7. The Creative Team will then present their strategy and tactics to the Account Team and the class during a class meeting.

Chapter Exercises

Exercise 2: Tactical Integration Mapping

This is a technique of graphic visualization used to plan the interactions, measurements, evaluation, analytics, and tracking of the effectiveness of campaign components.

The purpose of Tactical Integration Mapping is to identify opportunities for consumer engagement, campaign integration, tactics that lack measurement, or additional **calls to action** for individual communications.

The Mapping process:

1. Following appropriate competitive and market research, and strategic planning, each student writes a list of proposed tactical campaign elements.

2. For each participating communicator (e.g., the "Marketer/Business" and the "Consumer" in B2C), the student draws a circle on the whiteboard (or flip chart page) and writes the name of the communicator (e.g., business, consumer, etc.) within the circle. These are referred to as **Nodes.**

3. The student then draws arrows connecting the **Nodes**. These arrows symbolize an action (e.g., marketer sends an email, marketer broadcasts a commercial, the recipient of an email clicks on an embedded link and is taken to the website home page) and are therefore referred to as **Directional Verbs.**

4. For each piece of communication, the student draws a rectangle on the whiteboard (or flip chart page) and writes the name of the element (e.g., postal direct mail, email, print ad, TV ad, etc.) within the rectangle. These are referred to as **Nouns**.

5. Students use different color markers to indicate different parts of a campaign. Or, if several students are participating in the exercise, then each student can use a different color marker to enable the instructor to see the relative participation of each student in the mapping process.

6. Other students are invited to contribute ideas for new elements and additional linkages.

7. The students then need to identify methods of actively driving the actions of the message recipients, such as incentives and calls to action within the communications.

8. The students need to identify appropriate and effective measurement methods for each of the **Directional Verbs.**

9. These measurements can be summarized in dashboard form.

On the following page, see the example of a whiteboard hand-drawn map and the refined version created in Adobe Illustrator that shows how the **Directional Verb** can be linked to a dashboard that summarizes the measurements..

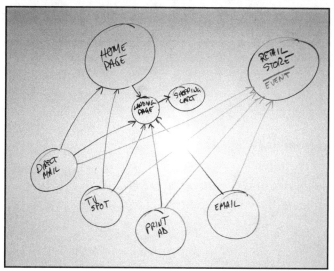

preliminary version

refined version

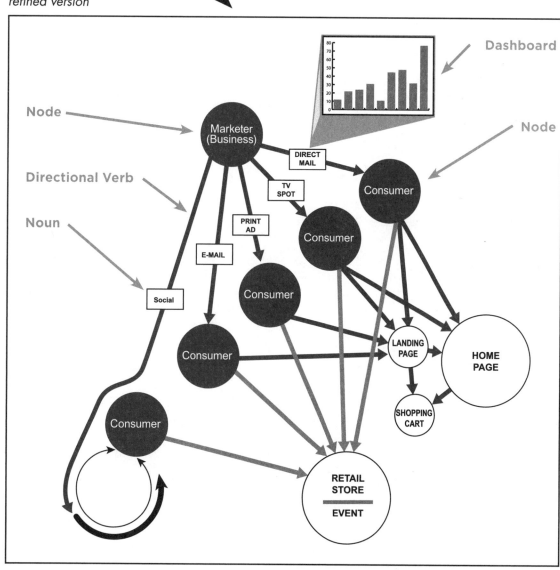

Dashboard

Node

Node

Directional Verb

Noun

Chapter Notes

1. "What Is Content Marketing?" (n.d.). Retrived from www. contentmarketinginstitute/what-is-content-marketing
2. Car Ownership in U.S. Cities Map (n.d.). Retrieved from www.governing. com/gov-data/car-ownership-numbers-of-vehicles-by-city-map.html

Chapter 5

How Advertising and Marketing Communications Are Made

The Creative Team Process; or
How the Creatives Make the Stuff the Suits Sell

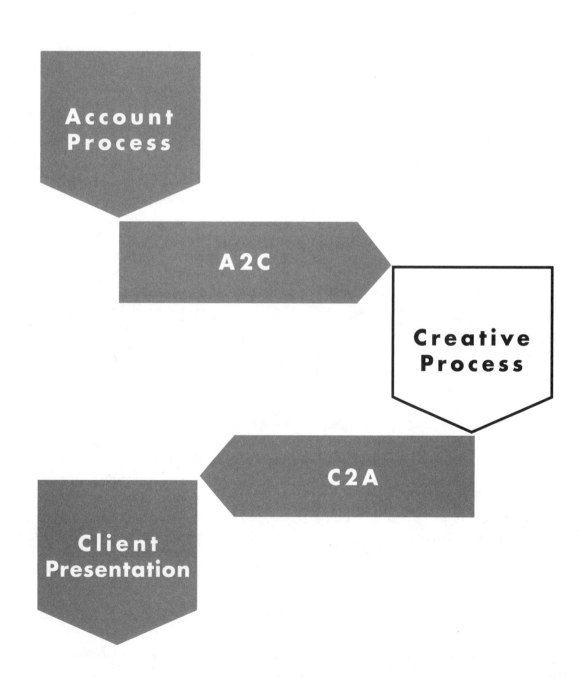

Introduction: How Advertising and Marketing Communications Are Made

The Creative Team Process; or How the Creatives Make the Stuff the Suits Sell

"The client wants to announce the launch of their new hi-tech spark plug," said Bill the account executive.

"Great!" I replied. "Are we launching this to the installers or their customers?"

"Both," replied Bill. "With one brochure."

"One brochure to launch a new product to two different target audiences, one B2B and the other B2C?" I asked.

"Yes," said Bill.

"Do you have any research from the client? Are their installers satisfied with the current products? Are they anticipating a new technology? Are their customers demanding newer spark plug tech in their cars?" I asked.

"The client expects us to find out," replied Bill. "What is our budget for research?" I asked.

"We don't have one," replied Bill.

"Tell you what, Bill," I suggested. "I know a few installers. Let's go and talk to them."

When we returned from our visits, I wrote up our interviews, and incorporated the insights we gained into the creative brief, and designed a solution to present.

Bill and I presented this brief and a concept to the client.

"What we discovered in our interviews was that the installers didn't even know about the last generation of spark plug, let alone the newest development in spark plug technology," I explained. "Furthermore, their customers don't specify the brand of spark plug or the type. Most customers rely on the installer to pick the appropriate part for their car."

"The new technology cannot simply be announced, but rather has to be positioned as part of the history of the company's leadership in spark plugs," I continued. "What we need is an education campaign to position your company as a leader in the past history of spark plugs, and the leader in technology for the future."

"How will you do that?" asked the client.

"Like this," I said, uncovering the presentation board with the layout.

"This concept is for a single brochure that presents historical information about your company's leadership, and technical data to the installers," I continued. "It then unfolds into a visually interesting time line showing the development of spark plugs over time, matches the type of plug technology to the era of car, and shows some other historical events happening at the same time."

"The time line can be displayed as an eye-catching poster in an installer's customer waiting room, where their customers can learn about the advantages of using your products. This will create a 'pull' demand from the customers, as well as a 'push' for your products from the installers," I concluded.

"OK," said the client. "Do it."

Many people who are not on the Creative Team assume that inspiration is the driving force behind breakthrough ideas, well-written copy, and effective visual design.

Rather than relying on inspiration, professional Creatives follow a process.

Learning and mastering the creative process is actually a principal objective of creative education for aspiring designers and copywriters.

Creative Process Steps

The creative process parallels and complements the account process. Both begin with *research* to gain a deep and thorough understanding of the situation and objectives, and the *problem* facing the client.

This is followed by developing *solutions*, *testing* and *refining* the solutions, and then *implementing* them.

Finally, the effectiveness of the solution must be *evaluated*.

Same Steps by Different Names

Many versions of the creative process have been defined, and most agencies define their own steps with proprietary names and details. However, these unique processes are all essentially based on the core steps of the creative process explained here.

For example, an agency might say their unique process is *Inquire, Insight, Inspire, Implement, Interpret.* Another version could be *Survey, Synthesize, Set Forth, Scrutinize.**

However, these steps are essentially the same as what I describe on the following pages of this chapter.

* These steps are examples, and not intended to represent any particular agency's process. Any resemblance is purely coincidental, but it would be really funny if an agency actually used these names for their steps.

Introduction: How Advertising and Marketing Communications Are Made

The Creative Team Process; or How the Creatives Make
the Stuff the Suits Sell

THE CREATIVE TEAM PROCESS

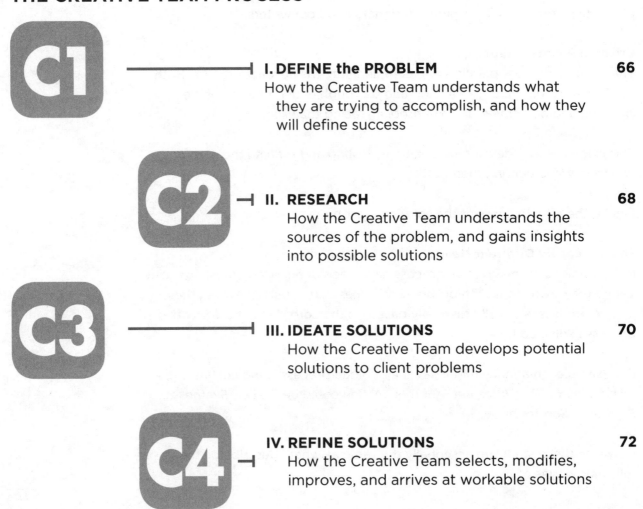

I. DEFINE the PROBLEM

How the Creative Team understands what they are trying to accomplish,
and how they will define success

As mentioned in The WRONG PRESCRIPTION Problem, p. 102, and The TAKING THE WRONG PRESCRIPTION Problem, p. 148, the client will sometimes ask for a specific tactical execution because they think they already know how to solve their business problems or competitive situation.

Too often, however, the tactic that the client requests will not solve the problem they presume exists. Furthermore, the problem they presume exists is often not the problem that they really are facing.

Therefore, a clear and accurate definition of the problem is essential to being able to develop an effective solution.

In order to arrive at a clear definition of a problem, additional creative specific research is often required (see **Step II. Research**, p. 68).

Consequently, the first two steps of the creative process are iterative. These steps are repeated as necessary to gain relevant insights into the causes of and solutions to the real problems and challenges facing their client.

Problem Definition Steps

The process of defining the specific problem or set of problems is different for the Creative Team than for the Account Team, but these two processes and objectives are closely related.

While the Account Team will help the client define their business problem, the challenge for the Creative Team is to define the problem as a strategic and tactical communications issue.

This process of translating the business issue into a creative issue is often challenging.

Not all business problems can be solved by advertising or marketing communications. It is not in an agency's interest to accept responsibility for changing a company's fortunes when the company has issues that are outside the scope of marketing communications to solve.

For example, a quality problem with a company's suppliers must be fixed by the company, either by changing suppliers or by effecting better processes at the supplier or employing other quality-control methods.

If an agency accepts the challenge of communicating to the client's customers the idea that quality problems have been addressed, but does so before the problems have actually been resolved, this will not solve the company's problems. The result will be that the agency may be scapegoated, and the agency's reputation can suffer.

Steps to take:
1. Examine the business issues as described in the **Creative Brief**.
2. Can the business issue be solved by the agency?
   a. If no, then the agency can advise, but probably can't help.
   b. If yes, then the solution needs to be matched to the issue.

While this diagram is not comprehensive, it does show some divisions between and overlaps of Business, Marketing, and Advertising/Marketing Communications/Strategy areas.

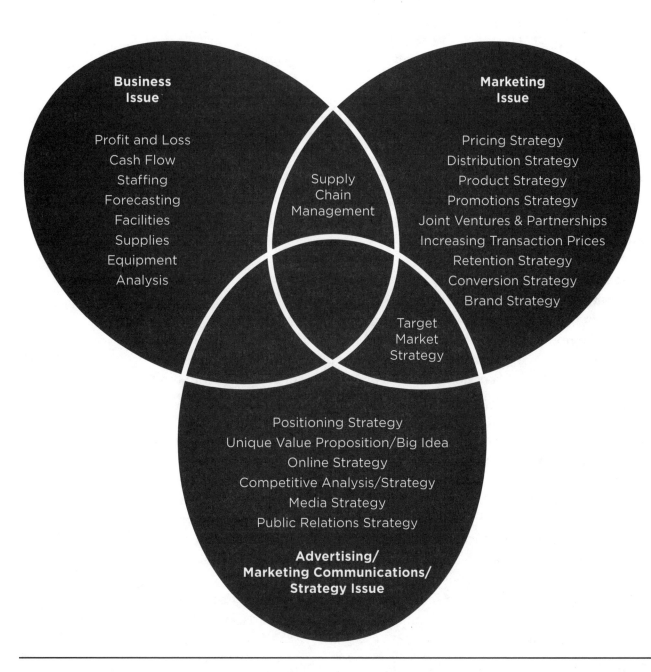

Business Issue

Profit and Loss
Cash Flow
Staffing
Forecasting
Facilities
Supplies
Equipment
Analysis

Supply Chain Management

Marketing Issue

Pricing Strategy
Distribution Strategy
Product Strategy
Promotions Strategy
Joint Ventures & Partnerships
Increasing Transaction Prices
Retention Strategy
Conversion Strategy
Brand Strategy

Target Market Strategy

Positioning Strategy
Unique Value Proposition/Big Idea
Online Strategy
Competitive Analysis/Strategy
Media Strategy
Public Relations Strategy

**Advertising/
Marketing Communications/
Strategy Issue**

II. RESEARCH

How the Creative Team understands the sources of the problem, and gains insights into possible solutions

In addition to using information provided by the client, the Creative Team conducts analysis and research in order to better comprehend the client's situation, the marketplace environment, and the objectives of a campaign.

Creative Research

The research that the Creative Team undertakes is different from that of the Account Team. The objectives of Creative Team research are focused on understanding:

- customer motivations
- strategy and tactics behind the client's previous marketing communications
- marketing communications strategy and tactics of the client's direct competition
- the larger environment of marketing communications, referred to as "clutter" or "noise," through which the Creative Team's solution must effectively reach the intended audiences

Research is an essential step to gain an understanding of the client's situation, challenges, and the underlying causes of their problems (see **The WRONG PRESCRIPTION Problem**, p. 102).

Research Focus

The methods of Creative Team research include:

Client Communications Audit

The comprehensive, systematic evaluation of an organization's external and internal communications to answer essential questions. For example;

- What has the client done over their history to communicate with the customers? With their employees?
- What is the client currently doing to communicate?
- What are the communications-method preferences of their external and internal audiences?
- How well are the current communications working?
- Is there a comprehensive communications plan? How well is it working?
- What are the important written messages of the communications?
- What are the important visual elements of the communication?
- How consistent and integrated are the communications?
- Are the communications focused on features or benefits?

As needed, other questions should be asked about timing, effectiveness, compliance across the organization with defined standards, and organizational support.

Competitive Communications Audit

This is a comprehensive, systematic evaluation of the communications from the client company's competitors, in order to answer essential questions:

- Who are the principal competitors?
- What are they doing to communicate? How well is this working?
- What are the important written messages of the competitive communications?
- What are the important visual elements of the communication?
- How consistent and integrated are the communications?
- Are the communications focused on features or benefits?

Research Methods

Several methods of qualitative and quantitative research are employed in a comprehensive communications audit. These include:

Document Review

The collection, examination, and description of all current and past communications (described above in Communications Audit)

Internal Review

Surveying and interviewing employees and management regarding their knowledge of the key messages of internal and external communications, and the effectiveness of those efforts.

External Review

Surveying, interviewing, and conducting focus groups with current and past customers, and other relevant publics, regarding their knowledge of the key messages of the company's communications, their recall of those messages, the effectiveness of those efforts, and their perceptions of the client's brand.

Research Results

The results of the Creative Team research can indicate the need to change the Problem Definition (see step I. Define the Problem, p. 66). Consequently, the first two steps of the Creative Process are iterative, and repeated as necessary to gain the required insights.

III. IDEATE SOLUTIONS

How the Creative Team develops potential solutions to client problems

Ideation, a portmanteau of the words **idea**s and crea**tion**, is a term for the creation of new concepts. The expression of these concepts in words and images is the result of the Ideation Process.

Ideation Steps

Ideation occurs in two steps, Concept Development, and Concept Representation.

1. **Concept Development**

   In this step the creative team employs a variety of methods to develop many possible solutions to the problems identified in Step 1, while incorporating the results of the research conducted in Step 2. See the Ideation Methods below.

2. **Concept Representation**

   In order for the concepts to be presented to other members of the creative supervision and other members of the creative team for review and discussion, art directors and copywriters create written and visual representations of those concepts. ➤

   These representations are often referred to as roughs, comps (for comprehensive layout), or supercomps (made to resemble as much as possible how the actual produced, finished work will appear).

   NOTE:
   At this stage, an art director or designer who is not making marks on the page, and a copywriter who is not putting words on the page, are not concepting. They are only thinking about concepting.

Ideation Methods

Methods of ideation, include:

- **Convergent Thinking**

  This is a thinking process that follows defined logical steps to arrive at one correct solution. This method was first referred to as convergent thinking by psychologist J.P. Guilford,[1] and is appropriate during the creative process when the problem is straightforward, such as on a multiple-choice test. When a problem can be solved by convergent thinking, the likelihood is that a **Work Order** (see The WORK ORDER Problem, p. 100) is more appropriate than a Creative Brief (see p. 126)

- **Divergent Thinking**

  Also first described by psychologist J.P. Guilford,[2] divergent thinking refers to a creative thinking process employed to develop many possible solutions to a problem.

Some ideation methods that use divergent thinking include:

- **Brainstorming**

  A method of creative idea generation by a group in order to solve a problem, this technique was first described by Alex Osborn in his 1953 book *Applied Imagination*.[3] Osborn was a founding member of the agency BBDO (the O is for Osborn). See also **Osborn's Checklist** on p. 80 for a useful ideation tool, and the Chapter Exercise starting on page 82.

Brainstorming has two distinct stages:

- **Idea Generation**

  In the first phase, and after being informed about the problem, the group suggests ideas. The ideas are stated for all to hear, and the moderator writes the ideas on a whiteboard or large paper where they can be seen by all, since one idea may lead to another, and yet another after that. In this phase, no criticism or evaluation is allowed (i.e., there is no such thing as a bad idea). Even non-verbal naysaying is not allowed. People are encouraged to generate a large number of ideas, but the real value and focus is to build on other people's suggestions. This building effect is where the real value of brainstorming occurs.

- **Idea Combination, Evaluation, and Selection**

  In this phase, similar ideas are combined. Then the ideas are evaluated according to criteria developed by the group. Finally, several ideas are selected for Concept Representation by the art director and copywriter, and other members of the Creative Team as necessary.

Other Brainstorming techniques include:

- **Brainwriting**

  A term for methods that involve the participants writing several ideas, then passing them to the next participant, or posting them on a wall for all to see and then to vote for in the evaluation stage. One of the possible advantages of brainwriting is that people who are less outgoing may feel more able to contribute than they would during a classic group Brainstorming session.

- **Reverse Brainstorming**

  A technique where the objective is to brainstorm the opposite of the solution to the stated problem. Asking how the problem could be made worse will often spark ideas for how to solve the problem.

A related technique:

- **Mind Mapping**

  The term mind map was popularized by Tony Buzan,[4] and is a method of diagramming information using a visual branching from a central word to other related word and images. Mind mapping emphasizes the use of images, symbols, and colors.

IV. REFINE SOLUTIONS

How the Creative Team selects, modifies, improves, and arrives at workable solutions

Once the Concept Representations from Step 3 have been produced, presented, and commented upon by the Creative Director, the next step is to refine these concepts.

NOTE:

This refinement step refers to the presentation and commenting *within* the Creative Team. This internal team process *usually* occurs before the Creative Team briefing to the Account Team (C2A).

However, it is possible, and even preferred, that some members of the Account Team remain involved at preliminary stages. If these account people are "creative savvy" and can be active contributors to the creative process, then their ongoing involvement can meaningfully contribute to a more effective solution.

Presenting preliminary solutions to the Account Team can help to get their buy-in to the proposed solutions. Consequently, this step could be represented in this way.

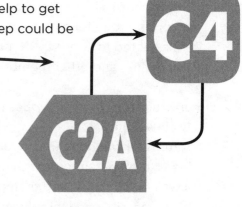

Solution Refinement Steps

1. Internal presentation and discussion with Creative Director and other members of Creative and Account Teams as necessary.
2. Art Director and Copywriter, and other Creative Team members as necessary, incorporate the changes and modifications from the Creative Director.
3. If necessary, the Art Director and Copywriter start another round of Ideation, literally returning to the "drawing board."
4. The Art Director and Copywriter repeat Refinement Step 1, as needed until viable, approved solutions are achieved.

NOTE:

Yes, I know that actual drawing boards are not much used, although I do require design students to begin their thinking with pencil and paper, or digital tablet and stylus. However, "returning to the screen" lacks the same meaning and context.

Solution Refinement Methods

For the work that has been presented:

1. Incorporate all copy changes required by the Creative Director.
2. Incorporate all design changes required by the Creative Director.
3. The Art Director and the Copywriter collaborate to make sure the words and images work well together.
4. Produce new concept representations (comps).
5. Re-present to the Creative Director.
6. Repeat as necessary.

For going back to the drawing board:

1. Conduct additional research as needed.
2. Begin the Ideation process again, to develop new concepts using alternative Brainstorming methods.
3. Select the most viable concepts.
4. Produce new concept representations (comps).
5. Re-present to the Creative Director.
6. Repeat as necessary.

V. TEST SOLUTIONS

How the Creative Team evaluates solutions before implementation

Testing solutions before they are deployed or implemented is an essential part of assuring that the marketing communications will have the intended effect. Whether increasing consumer awareness or driving purchase (see Purchase Funnel, p. 53 and p. 107), the solutions should be tested before final selection and approval.

However, sometimes the only pretesting are the reactions and professional judgement of the experienced Creative Director and Account Team management. Some successful campaigns did not do well in pretesting.[5]

Pretesting should inform, but not dictate, the creative solution. Every pretesting method has pros and cons.

A FEW SOLUTIONS–TESTING METHODS

While there are too many methods of pretesting available to describe here, these examples illustrate the purpose of pretesting and the basic approach.

A/B Testing – Incoming

Website visitor traffic gets directed equally to two versions of a website. Each site visitor sees only one version of the site. Each visitor's interaction with the site is tracked and evaluated.

Comparing two versions of a website in this way enables an understanding of which site version will deliver better results such as time on site (i.e., **stickiness**) and **conversion** (turning a site visitor into a purchaser).

Many elements of the site can be tested, including copy, images, and layout.

A/B Testing – Outgoing

A method of email subject line testing where a small test sample of a final emailing list is selected. This sample group is split into two, with each half receiving an email with a different version of the subject line. The version that is opened most, and has the most click-throughs, and ultimately the best conversion, will then be applied to the entire email list for deployment.

Multivariate Testing

Similar to A/B testing where only two variables are tested, multivariate testing compares a larger number of variables to test how these elements interact in context. Multivariate testing of a website requires a large volume of site traffic to be directed to each version in order to acquire enough data to successfully evaluate each combination of tested elements.

Quantitative and Qualitative

While many methods are quantitative, resulting in specific numerical results, some methods are qualitative, resulting in information about the thoughts and feelings of members of the target audience.

It can be useful to think of quantitative testing as measuring actions, while qualitative testing measures thoughts and feelings.

Focus Groups

The traditional focus group is a select number of people assembled in a room, directed in a discussion by a moderator, and monitored through mirrored glass by a team of observers.

The focus group is asked questions, and led by the moderator in their discussion of the subject in order to reveal insights into the target audience's reactions and preferences. The subject of the testing can be anything from a proposed advertising campaign, to a new brand name or visual identity, a slogan, or any other element of marketing communications.

However, a focus group has risks, and can unintentionally mislead observers who take the participants' comments as prescriptive rather than as indicative. The participants generally can tell you what they don't like, but they are not effective at directing what the agency or company should do. Also, in a situation such as a focus group, most people have a desire to participate and contribute something worthwhile. Consequently, participants may make up answers rather than feel embarassed by having no opinion.[6]

Finally, if the participants do not accurately represent the target audience, or the moderator is insufficiently skilled, the results of the focus group can be misleading.

VI. IMPLEMENT/PRODUCE SOLUTIONS

How the Creative Team produces, implements, and deploys a solution

Following internal creative department evaluation, Account Team reaction and comments, and pretesting, the solutions will be revised, and retested as necessary. Once the proposed solution has reached a final production version, it must then be produced.

Specific methods of production are used for different types of marketing communications. There are too many production methods involved to describe here, however the following examples illustrate this step of the creative process.

Larger agencies generally have production departments to execute these final stages of the process in addition to the Creative Team that concepted, wrote, designed, and shot the work. However, this stage is still part of the Creative process, and generally includes additional approvals from the Creative Team, the Account Team, and the clients.

Print
Print marketing communications includes a wide variety of executions, ranging in size from as small as a business card to as large as a billboard. Print includes magazine advertising, brochures, catalogs, billboards, business cards, sales training materials, and more. Each type of execution employs specific technologies, including sheet fed and web presses, and offset and digital printing. Furthermore, each type has specific technical requirements, including dimensions, resolution, and file type.

While the specifics of production vary according to the requirements of each type of media, there are some common steps in this part of the creative process:

- Proofreading: checking for errors that a spell-checking function can't identify
- Preflighting: checking for errors in file preparation
- Packaging: assembling the collection of files and resources necessary to print correctly
- Proofing: reviewing a printed sample that reflects the final "as printed" version
- Press checks: reviewing and approving the final version as it comes off the printing press

Web

At the final deployment stage of web development, the site has already been through planning, design, development, functionality testing, and approval. Now the site requires a few more steps to be launched and available to the intended audience:

- Final tweaks: small changes are made for improving the look and functionality of the site, without necessitating an additional round of approvals
- Transfer to live server: the site is moved from a development server to a "live" server
- Testing: diagnostic tools are used to validate the links and the code
- Browser checking: the site is again checked for functionality and appearance in several browsers. This checking also occurs earlier in the process.

Video (Post-Production)

The final stage in the process of creating TV commercials and other forms of video is referred to as Post-Production. This is a rough outline of the post-production steps:

- Editing – Initial Assembly: selected elements from the shoot are assembled in the rough order following the approved storyboard
- Editing – Rough Cut: the initial assembly is adjusted, additional elements may be added, rough sound is added, and rough effects and titles are added.
- Editing – Final Cut: the rough cut is refined, put into the final sequence, and the timing is adjusted to its final form
- Effects and color: motion graphics and visual effects are added, and the color is adjusted and enhanced (referred to as color grading)
- Final Audio: depending on the application, the sound including music, effects, and dialogue will be mixed to final levels and format
- Variations: many TV commercials have local market identifiers added at the end, including local company names, phone numbers, and URLs
- Mastering: the final digital version is produced for delivery

VII. MEASURE RESULTS

How the Creative Team works with the Account Team to see how well the intended results were achieved

Measuring and Evaluating the results of your efforts are the essential final steps of the creative process. This step enables the Creative Team to prove their success, and the Account Team to prove the value of the agency's work.

The success of the efforts must be stated in reference to the problems that were identified as the first step of the process (see p. 66, **I. Define the Problem**). Since the creative work was developed and produced with a specific problem in mind, the work is only effective if it solves that problem.

This reference back to the original problem definition guides how the results will be evaluated.

There are two parts of this step: **Measurement** and **Evaluation**.

Measurement refers to the collection of the actual performance data of each tactical execution. For example, what was the response rate (numerically stated) of a piece of direct marketing (tactical execution).

Evaluation refers to the assessment of the measurement. How well did the execution perform with respect to the objectives?

Measurement:
For example, if the original problem was one of a slipping market share, did the campaign stop the decrease, or actually increase market share? The measurement states in numerical terms by how much the share increased.

If the defined problem was to reach a new market segment, did the campaign bring in those new customers? How many?

If the problem was defined in the SWOT as an external Threat, for example from a rising competitor, did the campaign successfully diminish the threat by improving the brand perception of the client company?

The measurement of the final results cannot however, stand alone. A campaign, for example, is a complex effort that depends on the many component parts and steps that build to the overall success.

Therefore, the Creative Team must build into each tactical execution the capability for measurement. Each of these component measurements enables the team to identify underperfoming links in the campaign, in order to adjust them or reallocate the budget and resources away from those elements.

How will you identify and correct weaknesses in the chain of marketing activities that combine to create a successful campaign overall?

Importance of Results to the Creative Portfolio

The calculation of the Return on Marketing Investment is often performed by the Account Team. However, these results are of critical relevance to the Creative Team as well.

An effective framework for presenting a creative portfolio, by an individual or an agency, is based on this creative process. Each example of work is presented with an explanation of The Situation (i.e., Step I. The Problem Definition), The Solution (i.e., Step VI. The Solution), and Results (i.e., Step VII. Measure Results). In order to format a portfolio in this way, a Creative needs to know and be able to state the effectiveness of their work.

Results Evaluation Formulae

Two relevant formulae are Return on Marketing Investment (ROMI) and Short-Term ROMI. These are not the only measures of effectiveness, but are recognized as significant.

ROMI calculates the overall effectiveness of a campaign.

$$\frac{\text{Gross Profit} - \text{Marketing Investment}}{\text{Marketing Investment}} = \text{ROMI}$$

Short-Term ROMI calculates the effectiveness of an individual marketing tactical execution.

$$\frac{\text{Incremental Revenue Attributable to Marketing Activity}}{\text{Marketing Activity Expenditure}} = \text{Short-Term ROMI}$$

Osborn's Checklist Plus

A useful tool for sparking creative thinking

In 1957, Alex Osborn not only developed Brainstorming (see Step 3, Ideate Solutions, p. 70). He also developed this checklist.[7] This checklist can be applied to problem solving to provoke original thinking.

Use each item to consider alternative ideas and variations in your process of creative thinking.

Osborn's Checklist

- **Put to other uses**
  - How can you use this in new ways?
  - How could it be used as it is?
  - What about with modifications?
- **Adapt**
  - How can you adapt this to different situations and circumstances?
  - What happens then?
- **Modify**
  - How can you change the elements?
  - Color, shape, form, position, substance, movement, sound?
- **Magnify**
  - What elements can you add to or enlarge?
  - Duration, frequency, height, length, strength, exaggeration, multiplication, scale?
- **Minify** [sic]
  - Can you remove or reduce elements?
  - Smaller, lower, shorter, lighter in color or value, removed, separated?

- **Substitute**
  - What elements can be changed?
  - Materials, processes, words, images, color, place?
- **Rearrange**
  - What elements can be moved around?
  - Patterns, components, sequence, timing?
- **Reverse**
  - What elements can be reversed, individually or in combination?
- **Combine**
  - Combine the components of this into something new.
  - Combine this with something similar.
  - Combine this with something different.

On the following page is a business card-sized reference I have carried since I was a student. When my thinking gets "stuck" I refer to this card for ways to spark my creative thinking. The card include Osborn's Checklist plus a list of the **Elements of Design,** which are the components of visual communication, and the **Principles of Design**, which are how the elements are organized. I have included a brief explanation of each of the elements and principles; I have not included the subject of typography, which is too complex a subject to cover here.

OSBORN'S CHECKLIST

ELEMENTS OF DESIGN*

- **Dot**
  A single mark in space with a precise position. Establishes the relation between negative and positive space
- **Line**
  A mark with greater length than width. Can be horizontal, vertical or diagonal, straight or curved, thick or thin.
- **Shape**
  Two-dimensional enclosed area, with width and length, can be geometric or organic
- **Form**
  Three-dimensional object, with width, length, and height
- **Space**
  Refers to perspective (the illusion of depth) and also to the area between and around objects (positive and negative space)
- **Color**
  The qualities of hue, value, and intensity or saturation
- **Texture**
  Surface quality, either actual or in appearance
- **Motion**
  Real-time moving images such as video

FOR A CREATIVE SOLUTION
- put to other uses
- adapt
- modify
- magnify
- minify
- substitute
- rearrange
- reverse
- combine

ELEMENTS OF DESIGN
- dot
- line
- shape
- form
- space
- color
- texture
- motion

PRINCIPLES OF DESIGN
- balance
- emphasis
- movement
- proportion
- pattern (repetition)
- rhythm
- unity
- variety
- gestalt
  - similarity
  - proximity
  - continuity
  - closure
  - equilibrium
  - common fate

GESTALT PRINCIPLES

- **Grouping by Similarity**
  Viewer sees similar elements as belonging together
- **Grouping by Proximity**
  Viewer sees closer elements as belonging together
- **Continuity**
  Implied continuation of lines or shapes
- **Closure**
  Mental completion between non-touching elements
- **Equilibrium**
  Preference for simplicity, stability
- **Common Fate**
  Elements with the same apparent direction are perceived as a unit

PRINCIPLES OF DESIGN*

- **Balance**
  Sense of stability, symmetrical or asymmetrical
- **Emphasis**
  Calling attention to important elements by contrast with other elements
- **Movement**
  The path a viewer's eye follows rather than real-time motion
- **Proportion**
  Relative size and scale of elements
- **Pattern**
  Repetition of any of the elements
- **Rhythm**
  Starts, stops, and pauses of the viewer's eye movement in response to the placement and use of Elements of Design
- **Unity**
  Organized relationship among elements so they function together
- **Variety**
  Changing the character of elements to create interest

* The earliest reference to the Elements and Principles of Design that I have found is Maitland Graves' 1951 book "Art of Color and Design."[8] There may be an earlier definition of these terms.

The Creative Team Process Exercise

Exercise: Classic Group Brainstorming

Brainstorming requires a facilitator, who could be the instructor or a student. It is useful to repeat this exercise so that several students can gain experience as a facilitator.

Also required are:

*   whiteboards and dry erase markers in a variety of colors and/or flip chart paper pads
*   non-marring tape such as painter's tape, or push pins (if allowed to be used on the walls of the room)

Step 1: Identify a problem to be solved.

The problem can be suggested by a student or the instructor, and can be based on a current project or assignment, or a real company example or case study.

In an agency or business setting, the participants should* be given all the background information in advance so that they come to the Brainstorm as informed about the problem as possible. Therefore, student participants should also read background information, such as a case study, in advance of the Brainstorm session.

The problem can be as simple as "What do we name a company?" or as challenging as "How do we bring more people into a store."

The problem is written on the whiteboard for everyone to see.

Step 2: Idea Generation

2.1 The Brain Dump

It is expected that while reading the background information about a problem prior to the Brainstorm, the participants will have individual ideas about possible solutions.

* For a brainstorm to be effective, the participants should come to the session informed about the situation. However, this is an ideal that does not always occur. Similarly, even when participants do receive information in advance, often not all of them actually read the information before the meeting.

Just as in The CRUSH DURING KICKOFF Problem (see p. 118), it is important to retrieve these ideas from everyone as a first step. Since it is akin to opening up your head and dumping a brain full of ideas onto the wall, this step is called a **Brain Dump.** While this term sounds pejorative, it is not meant to be, since some of these ideas may be useful.

The participants' ideas are stated for everyone to hear. The moderator writes the ideas on a whiteboard or large paper where they can be seen by all, since one idea may lead to another, and yet another after that. In this phase, no criticism or evaluation is allowed (i.e., there is no such thing as a bad idea). Even non-verbal naysaying is not allowed. People are encouraged to generate a large number of ideas, but the real value and focus is to build on other people's suggestions. This building effect is where the real value of brainstorming occurs.

The Parking Lot (see p. 119 for directions on creating your own individual Parking Lot)

During a Brainstorm, the participants will often suggest ideas that apply to different aspects of the situation, or are relevant for another discussion, or are jumping ahead to a suggestion of tactics before the strategy is determined. While these are not "bad" ideas, especially during the Idea Generation step, it is useful to capture these ideas on a separate flip chart page used for this purpose. This "Parking Lot" of ideas should be retained, and may be revisited during a later stage of the Brainstorm or creative process.

2.2 The Unsticking

Once the participants have stated the ideas that they have brought to the Brainstorm, and have started to build on each other's ideas, the suggestions will slow or even stop completely. When the participants get "stuck," it is time for the facilitator to use any of a variety of techniques to restart the Brainstorm.

Osborn's Checklist (see pp. 80-81) is one useful tool for the facilitator. By applying the questions suggested by the checklist, the participants' creative thinking will often become "unstuck."

Step 3: Idea Combination, Evaluation, and Selection

In this phase, similar or related ideas are combined. This step can also lead to the generation of even more ideas, as the combination of different elements suggested can lead to more new ideas. Often during this step, suggestions for refining the combined ideas are offered.

The Creative Team Process Exercises

Step 4: Evaluation

Though the first steps of the Brainstorm are done without criticism, and a large number of ideas are developed, eventually the ideas that have the most potential for effectiveness must be selected and evaluated.

The 5X5 Evaluation Method

One method of evaluation begins with creating a table grid. On the left, defining the rows, are various criteria agreed upon by the group. Each of these criteria can have a multiplier based on the relative importance of the criterion. For example, one factor may be twice as important as another. This relative value would be indicated by a 2x next to the item.

Along the top of the grid are the five consensus choices for evaluation, each heading one of the columns.

The group rates each choice on a 1 to 5 scale by each criterion. The votes for each choice for each criterion are totaled and multiplied (if needed), and the total is placed in the appropriate box. The numbers for each choice are totaled at the bottom of each column.

The number total is indicative, but not determinative, of the solution that the group considers most likely to be effective.

	Choice 1	Choice 2	Choice 3	Choice 4	Choice 5
Criteria A 2X					
Criteria B					
Criteria C					
Criteria D 1.5 X					
Criteria E					
TOTAL					

Conclusion

The two biggest errors made in Brainstorming are being critical during the Idea Generation Step, and not being critical during the Evaluation Step. These steps are both essential to the utility of Brainstorming.

Chapter Notes

1. Guildford, J. P. (1967). *The Nature of Human Intelligence*. New York: McGraw-Hill.

2. Ibid.

3. Osborn, Alex. (1953). *Applied Imagination: Principles and Procedures of Creative Problem Solving.* New York: Charles Scribner's Sons.

4. Buzan, T. & Buzan, B. (1996). *The Mind Map Book: How to Use Radiant Thinking to Maximize Your Brain's Untapped Potential* (reprint edition) New York: Plume.

5. McKee, Steve. (2007). *Beware the Advertising Pretest.* Retrieved from http://www.bloomberg.com/news/articles/2007-12-07/beware-the-advertising-pretestbusinessweek-business-news-stock-market-and-financial-advice

6. Krueger, R. & Casey, M.A. (2015). *Focus Groups, A Practical Guide for Applied Research.* Thousand Oaks, CA: SAGE Publications.

7. Osborn, Alex. (1953). *Applied Imagination: Principles and Procedures of Creative Problem Solving.* New York: Charles Scribner's Sons.

8. Graves, Maitland. (1951). *Art of Color and Design*. New York. McGraw-Hill. Second Edition edition (1951)

Chapter 6

The Road to Successful Collaboration
The Cross-Discipline Process Flow

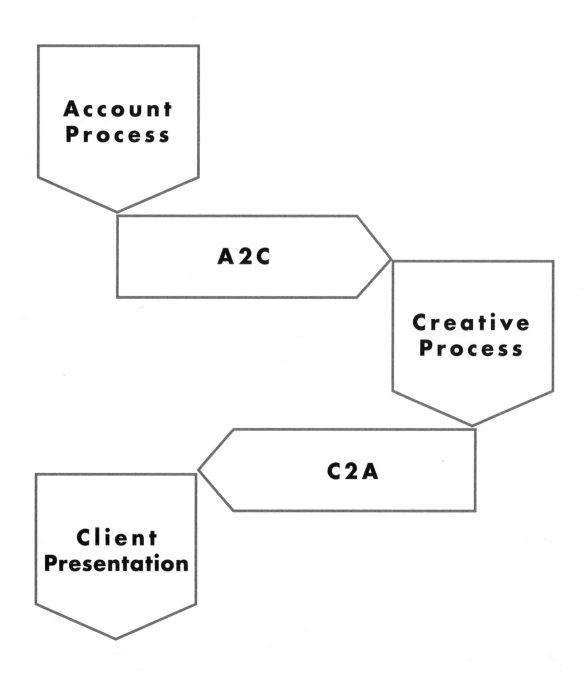

Introduction:
The Road to Successful Collaboration

The Cross-Discipline Process Flow

"Why did you write this memo?" asked Jaime, the account executive, angrily clutching a printed copy of the memo.

"I wrote the memo because the project information that Jim [the new account manager] presented at the kickoff meeting raised a lot of red flags for me. It was my responsibility to the agency to state my concerns up front, so that we could work together to prevent problems."

"That's NOT your job," stated Jaime emphatically.

"That's all of our jobs," I replied. "Besides, no one else was doing it."

"Well, this work will lead to other better work from this client. So in the future just stick to your work and leave the account decisions to us," said Jaime.

"First, this type of work doesn't lead to other 'better' work. Doing this type of work positions us as a provider of cheap labor to the client. That is detrimental to the agency's long-term brand. Second, I suggest that in the future you listen to the concerns of the people who actually have to produce the work," I replied. "Actually,

I suggest that you address my concerns now, before we lose a lot of time and money on what appears to be project-based work that will not yield suitable profit for the time and effort we will spend on it, and will tie up people I need to work on more profitable client business."

"Just mind your own business," said Jaime between clenched teeth.

"This is my business," I replied. "I have to assign and schedule the creative staff. If I assign our best people to work on this stuff, we may lose them to another firm."

"Creatives are replaceable," said Jaime. She then turned and walked away.

The project did turn out to be time and labor intensive, which the client was unwilling to pay for appropriately. I soon reassigned the art director and copywriter to other projects, and assigned less-experienced, less-costly people to work on Jaime's unprofitable project.

The flow of the work between the Account Team Process and the Creative Team Process is usually something like the diagram on the following pages.

There are of course variations depending on whether essential functions, such as media planning and buying, are in the same agency as the Creative Team, or are on the client side, or some other variation of these possibilities.

And, as the story on the preceding page illustrates, when one functional area of the agency doesn't fully understand the implications of their decisions to the other functional areas, there can be a disruption in collaboration.

As a part of the overall process, the Account Team briefs the Creative Team. Often this creative brief is actually a collaborative process itself between the Account Executive and the Creative Director, but this is not always the case.

The Creative Team begins their process, and then presents their work to the Account Team.

And finally the Account Team, along with the Creative Director and other members of the Creative Team as appropriate, will present the proposed work, campaign, and/or project to the client.

Because the creative brief should include the definition of the problem, and the objectives of the project or campaign, and have already been agreed to by the client, the presentations from the Creative Team to the Account Team, and to the client, are often referred to as **"selling to the brief."**

The briefing, and selling to the brief, are the process interfaces between the Account Team and the Creative Team where the process can often get off track.

The Cross-Discipline Process

How the work moves through the agency

Account Team Process

How the Account Team identifies opportunities

*See Chapter Four
Steps A1 to A6*

Iterative Process

Repeating the process as needed to develop effective solutions for the client

A2C

The ACCOUNT TEAM TO CREATIVE TEAM (A2C) BRIEFING Process
How the Account Team describes an opportunity to the Creative Team

See Chapter Seven

Account to Client Presentation

How the Account Team sells Creative solutions to the client

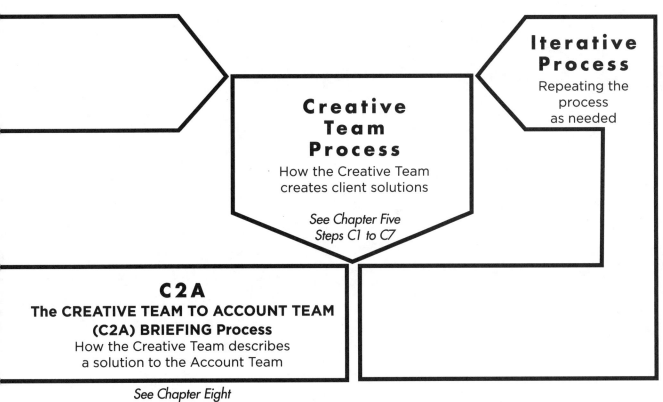

**Creative
Team
Process**

How the Creative Team
creates client solutions

*See Chapter Five
Steps C1 to C7*

**Iterative
Process**

Repeating the
process
as needed

C2A
**The CREATIVE TEAM TO ACCOUNT TEAM
(C2A) BRIEFING Process**
How the Creative Team describes
a solution to the Account Team

See Chapter Eight

Chapter 7

Account Team:
How to Help the Creatives
Make You a Hero to Your Client

The Nine Account Team + Two Creative Team Mistakes
That Can Happen During The A2C Briefing and After, and How To Fix Them

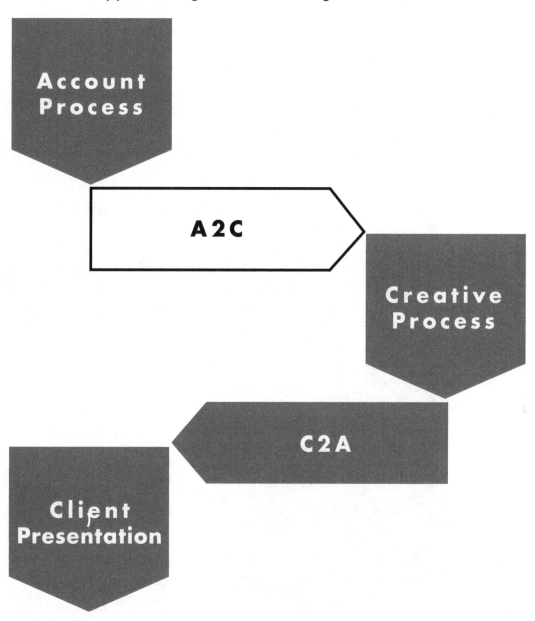

Introduction: The SUITS PLAY GOLF Problems

What goes wrong during the Creative Briefing (A2C) and after

Larry the account executive had just returned from a playing golf with a potential client. Larry walked into my office, and placed a cocktail napkin on my desk.

"Here it is!" said Larry excitedly.
"Um. Here's what, exactly?" I replied.
"Here's what the client wants."

I looked at the uneven, scribbles and bleeding ink on the napkin.

"How did you arrive at this…um…solution?" I asked, anticipating the answer.

"We were talking over drinks after golf, and we figured it out," said Larry.

"Just do it exactly like that," he exclaimed, pointing to the blurry scribble, "and the client will love it."

This story illustrates the problems that occur during the A2C Briefing, and is the reason I refer to them under the heading of **THE SUITS PLAY GOLF Problems**.

Among other problems, this story illustrates an account executive describing the tactics to be executed. I call this The WORK ORDER Problem, as if the brief is simply like an order to a fry cook in a diner.

What I have often found to happen in such a situation is that the tactics being "ordered" won't actually solve the client's problem. This is an example of The WRONG PRESCRIPTION Problem.

And when digging deeper, it becomes clear that the problem the client thinks they have is often not the problem they actually have. They have made The WRONG DIAGNOSIS. So it is important that the brief not dictate the solution, but describe the situation.

The SUITS PLAY GOLF category comprises eight mistakes including the WORK ORDER Problem, the WRONG PRESCRIPTION Problem, and the WRONG DIAGNOSIS Problem, and others.

The solutions to fixing the SUITS PLAY GOLF Problems are revealed by examining these component problems that occur during the A2C Briefing.

I describe solutions to each specific problem, and present exercises to develop the skills and practices to avoid these problems.

Additionally, solutions and exercises applicable to multiple problems can be found at the end of the chapter.

Introduction: The SUITS PLAY GOLF Problems

What goes wrong during the Creative Briefing (A2C) and after

THE ACCOUNT TEAM MISTAKES

Introduction: The SUITS PLAY GOLF Problems

What goes wrong during the Creative Briefing (A2C) and after

THE CREATIVE TEAM MISTAKES

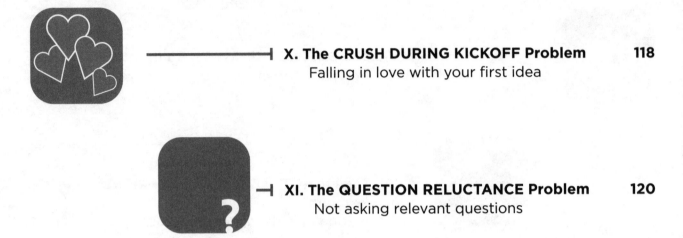

THE A2C BRIEFING SOLUTIONS

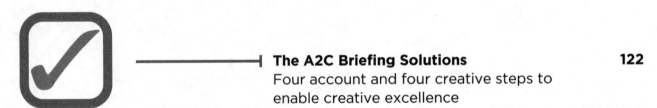

RESOURCES

I. The WORK ORDER Problem

Describing only the tactics to be executed

At the kickoff meeting for a new client project, account executive Bob placed a brochure on the conference room table.

"The client loves this, so all we need to do is copy this."

"Bob, this is our client's competitor's capabilities brochure," I pointed out.

"Well that's what the client wants," explained Bob, hoping in vain that this would end the discussion.

"What exactly did the client say, Bob?" I asked.

"He said that he needed to be as good as the competition," Bob answered.

"Doesn't our client actually want to be better than his competition? Much better? And if we only copy what his competition is doing, then he will only appear to be an imitator."
Bob started getting a pained look on his face, as he often did in these meetings.

"Did the client specifically ask for a new, glossy, capabilities brochure using special and expensive printing techniques? Isn't the client trying to reach a new, younger demographic?" You know, the ones with the smart phones, tablets, and gaming devices?"

"Tell you what Bob. You can tell your client, or better yet you can let me explain to him, how we will define a strategy to position his company as a leader and innovator in the field so that his brand will appeal to a new target audience, rather than being reduced to a low-priced commodity. This way he will be able to command a premium price for his superior brand."

"I think that will be OK. You should do that."

"Thanks, Bob. That's a great idea."

When the Account Team simply tells the Creative Team only what to do, as in the story above, listing the tactics to be executed (see The Difference Between Strategy and Tactics, p. 101) rather than describing the business problems that need to be solved, then the conversation of the briefing is little more than a **WORK ORDER.** This is similar to the directions given to a short order cook in a diner.

A work order may include some degree of discretion in the exact techniques used to accomplish a task, or may be specific and detailed to the tiniest element. Either way, a work order alone may be sufficient for making updates or changes to existing work, but is not appropriate as a means of collaborating to find a creative solution to a business problem.

The WORK ORDER Problem limits the possible creative solutions to ones that already exist.

Strategy and Tactics

A goal is a business objective, such as increasing market share, reaching new customers, or increasing sales to existing customers. Realistic goal setting depends on a company's marketplace position and finances, and whether the markets for their products or services are strong or weak.

A strategy is an idea (see UVPs and Big Ideas, p. 163), a concept of how those business goals could be achieved. A strategy could include defining a new use for an existing product, creating a new product category, or expanding into a new market.

Tactics are actions you take to execute the strategy. If you say, "we can use..." then you are describing a tactic. For example, "we can use...a billboard" or "We can use ...an e-mail campaign" then you are describing a tactic, not a strategy.

The Solution:

Provide a Creative Brief to the Creative Team that describes the client's business situation, background, context, competition, objectives, target audiences, stakeholders, and other pertinent information, but does not specify the answers. This allows the Creative Team to develop effective, innovative solutions (see pp. 126–127 for a sample Creative Brief).

The Problems/Solutions Exercise:

1. Divide into groups.
2. Each group quickly brainstorms a list of business problems, then chooses one.
3. Each group presents a business problem, without describing any solutions.
4. Each group's business problem is written on a whiteboard or large sheet of paper, and posted around the room.
5. Each group then brainstorms a list of possible solutions to one or more problems.
6. Each group presents their possible solutions. These solutions are aggregated under the posted problems.
7. The solutions are discussed and evaluated. Similar solutions are grouped together during this part of the process.

II. The WRONG PRESCRIPTION Problem

Suggesting tactics that won't solve the client's business problem

"We're so glad you are here. Welcome aboard!" said Joan and Jim, the account project managers, as they welcomed me to a new agency.

"Thanks," I replied. *"Glad to be here. Is there something I can help you with?"*

"Yes, actually," said Joan. *"The art director who left didn't finish this prepping the files for this direct mail piece, and we can't figure the complicated fold. Can you help?"*

"I'll be glad to take a look."

Later...

"Here you go. The files are organized and collected here, and this is a folding mock up for the printer to follow."

Joan and Jim happily looked at the detailed folding mock up.

"This is great!" they exclaimed.

"Thanks. This will print correctly now," I said. *"Too bad you won't get a good response."*

"Uh...what?" they both stammered, wide-eyed.

"Oh, I got the files and folds to work, but the messaging is incorrect, the images are confusing or off-target, and the call to action is hidden. This will not be an effective solution."

"What would you do differently?" they asked.

"Well, why don't we sit down and review the original Creative Brief, and discuss the possibilities..."

If you went to your family doctor complaining of athlete's foot, and the doctor prescribed cough medicine, this obviously would be the wrong prescription for your ailment.

Worse yet, if you went to your doctor complaining of a cough, and you demanded that you have your tonsils removed, this would be jumping to a conclusion without gaining a complete understanding of the situation.

While this is similar to the WORK ORDER Problem, in that the patient is dictating orders instead of describing symptoms, the **WRONG PRESCRIPTION Problem** often starts with an impatient "patient," i.e., the client.

Just as a physician must listen carefully to their patient, and must ask the right questions to determine the problem, an Account Team and a Creative Team must accurately determine the causes and current situation or else they will likely produce creative work that will not actually solve the client's real business problems. This is a WRONG PRESCRIPTION Problem.

The difference between
Marketing and Creative Strategies

Marketing strategies include the traditional "4 Ps" including Price, Place, Product, Promotion.

Promotion as one of the 4 Ps refers to marketing communications, including advertising. This is different from the specific sense of a "pricing" promotion such as a coupon or discount, which is included in the 4 Ps under Price.

The Promotion aspect of the 4 Ps encompasses creative strategy. **Creative strategy** *includes the "Big Idea," the unifying, innovative concept that drives the marketing efforts of a brand or product.*

The interface between the Marketing and Creative functions, seen as the overlap in the diagram, is represented by the Creative Brief.

A product's Unique Value Proposition (UVP) may seem to belong to the Product category, but the UVP is a Promotion strategy that is informed by the unique attributes of the Product.

The Solution:

Work with the Creative Team to develop a Creative Brief that describes the problem without dictating the solution.

The Creative Brief Exercise:

1. As a team, fill in the sample Creative Brief on pp. 126–127, and present the brief to another team. See what questions the other team asks, in order to improve your briefing process.

2. As a team, take the problem presentations from The WORK ORDER Problem Exercise (p. 101), and write them up in a Creative Brief format.

3. If you don't have enough information to lead to an actionable insight, do more research, and bring your additional insights to discuss in the next class.

4. Establish in the brief what you want the target audience *to think*, *to feel*, and *to do*.

III. The WRONG DIAGNOSIS Problem

Describing the wrong problem

Tim, an account project manager, sidled into my office.

"He's not happy," said Tim, referring to his boss John, the account executive.

"I'm sorry to hear that," I said. "And what is the cause of his distress?"

"He can't sell your work to the client."

"Let me talk to him." I offered. "Perhaps I can help."

Reluctantly, John agreed to meet.

The first 20 minutes were a profanity-laden tirade by John about the obstinacy of clients, the unfairness of life, and the problems caused by the Creatives.

When, at the end of his rant, he paused for a breath, I said, "If you are done for the moment, can I ask you a few questions?"

He agreed, and in a few questions I was able to determine that the brief upon which the creative work was based had presented the WRONG DIAGNOSIS of the client's problem.

John was trying to sell the client an incentive program. What the client actually needed was a culture change communication campaign, with program elements intended to incentivize the employees to understand and adopt the changes.

Once I had established the correct diagnosis, we were able to propose a solution that satisfied the client, and the program was successfully launched.

The errors of **The WORK ORDER Problem** and **The WRONG PRESCRIPTION Problem** can often be traced back to the **WRONG DIAGNOSIS.**

Sometimes a client will request specific creative work, thinking that they are asking for the solutions to their business problem.

Often, the solution they request will not solve the problem they think they have, and the problem they think they have is not the problem they actually have.

When the Account Team either assumes the **WRONG DIAGNOSIS**, or accepts the client's **WRONG DIAGNOSIS** as correct without question, then passes this along to the Creative Team as a work order, the result is ineffective work.

Ultimately, in addition to the Account Team potentially losing a client due to a poorly performing program, the Creative Team also may be held responsible for presenting an ineffective solution.

Work Orders and Start of Work Documents

The Creative Team will be presented with some combination of the documents from the Account Team necessary for the beginning of client work. Confusion can occur as to when to use each type of project description.

A Start of Work Document comes first, and encompasses the Scope of Work, i.e., what the agency will deliver for the fees charged. This includes a list of the deliverables (a term for the work products that the agency is to deliver.

A Work Order is used to describe updates (e.x., new product numbers), changes (e.x., copy edits), and how previously developed work is to be extended into additional versions (e.x., print ads with different dimensions).

The Solution:

Understand the situations where a Work Order will suffice (see How and When to Use Work Orders and Start of Work Documents on this page) and those where a complete Creative Brief is needed. Then apply those documents appropriately to the situation.

Examples of situations that would require a Work Order include when updates or changes are made to existing project work, or when an additional item of work is added to the original scope of the project (although this can present a problem as well. See p. 116, The Slippery Slope Problem)

The YOUR Creative Brief Exercises:

1. Using your own projects and production timeline (see p. 128–129), write a Start of Work, Work Order, and/or Creative Brief depending on the type of project.

2. As you proceed to work on your projects, write a Project Change Notification (see p. 116) whenever you need to add items.

3. Note on your original documents if you need to change your initial project descriptions or schedule, or need to change documents from a Work Order to a Creative Brief, or vice versa.

IV. The EVERY TOOL IS A HAMMER Problem

Prescribing a media-specific solution

"Why did you create something so different and difficult to produce?" asked Lester, the managing director of the agency.

"My solution won the account away from the incumbent agency," I replied. "If I hadn't come up with what I did, we wouldn't be having this conversation, because we wouldn't have won the account."

Lester opened his mouth to say something, then stopped. Bill the account executive and Jenny my boss appeared to be stifling laughter. I continued, "If we had only given them what their agency has been giving them, the client would have no reason to change.

"Besides," I continued. "I had a plan for how to produce this idea from the get go."

There is an old saying that "if the only tool you have is a hammer, then every problem looks like a nail."* Applied to advertising and marketing, that means that an agency that specializes in one type of media execution, such as TV advertising, often sees their specialty as the solution to every problem.

However, while a hammer can be used to open a can of peas, a hammer is not the best tool for the job.

The **EVERY TOOL IS A HAMMER Problem** is a type of **WRONG PRESCRIPTION Problem** that particularly afflicts clients, agencies, or individuals who have not kept current with technology or audience preferences. For example, a client company that has been successful in using newspaper advertising may see additional ads as the solution to declining sales if they have not recognized the decline of newspaper reading among younger consumers. Since the tool they have been using has been successful in the past, they continue to see that tool as the answer.

Specialty creative firms can also suffer from this problem, in believing that their particular forte is the solution to all problems.

Clients who have heard about, but do not understand fully, the latest development in marketing or advertising, may insist on that particular tactic, rather than relying on the expertise of their agency to recommend the tactics best suited to execute a strategy and achieve business objectives.

The term "media agnostic" is frequently used to refer to an agency or a person who seeks a solution without having a built-in preference for one tactical tool over another.

* This saying has been attributed in its current form to Abraham Maslow,[1] and in an earlier version called "The Law of the Instrument" to Abraham Kaplan.[2] The saying probably predates either of them by a hundred years or so.

Specific Tactics and the
~~Purchase~~ Brand Attitude Funnel

You will probably encounter the traditional purchase funnel in your studies. The funnel was a widely used model of the stages of consumer activity and decision making.

This traditional linear model is outdated with respect to the complexity of consumer actions and decisions today. However, the traditional purchase funnel can still be a useful model as a learning tool to begin understanding which specific marketing communications tactics are most appropriate to facilitate consumers' movement from one attitude state to the next. That is why the word Purchase is intentionally crossed out in the title, to indicate that the old model is no longer adequately descriptive.

For example, while advertising has generally been most effective at creating or increasing awareness, i.e. moving people from the Unaware stage to the Aware stage, now social media and other tools allow consumers to find a brand on their own. Price promotions traditionally have been more effective at moving people from Awareness to Consideration, or from Consideration to Intent to Purchase, depending on the price and type of product, and the timing of the offer.

For one updated version of a consumer attitude and decision pathway model, see p. 55.

- Advertising
- Social Media

- Direct Marketing
- Price Promotion

- Personal Selling

- Frequent Buyer Program

Unaware

Aware

Consideration

Intent to Purchase

Loyalty

The Solution:
Understand that giving the client what they need can be more important for developing and maintaining a long-term business relationship than giving them only what they ask for right now.

The Brand Attitude Funnel Exercise:
1. Develop a Creative Brief (see pp. 126–127) that defines the objectives and target audience for your project or campaign.

2. Determine where your target audience currently is on the Brand Attitude Funnel.

3. Decide which marketing communications tactics are most appropriate to both reach and retain the target audience, and to move them from their current place on the Funnel to the next stage and beyond.

4. Review the updated model on p. 53. Where do your proposed tactics fit into this newer model? Do you need to add or subtract tactics, or rearrange them?

V. The FORTUNE TELLER Problem

Providing insufficient information

Jack the account executive knocked on my open office door. "Got a sec?" he asked.

"How can I help you?" I replied.

"I need you to design something."

"Anything in particular?" I asked.

"One of those things that you do, like that thing you did for those other guys."

"I'm always glad to help you, Jack. But, of course, I do need a Creative Brief, a job number, and a budget before I begin. I'll look for the kickoff meeting notice."

"Well," Jack said with disappointment, "Now you're just being difficult."

While some of my students may say that I always know what they are thinking, I am not actually a fortune teller, a psychic, or a soothsayer.

Just as the Creatives need to master the language of business, the Account Team needs to have some understanding of the language and process of creative concepting, development, design, and production. One of the chief complaints from the Creative Team about briefs from the Account Team is the lack of sufficient information necessary to develop a media agnostic, creative solution to a business problem.

The Solution:
Follow the Creative Brief format. Provide all of the information needed. Asks lots of questions. Research the answers and the questions as needed. The client may not have the correct answers.

The Job Number/To Do List Exercise:
This exercise works in conjunction with the production planning calendar (see pp. 128–129), and begins to build the valuable skill of being able to estimate time by learning to record the actual time spent working on projects

1. Create a master list of class "**Job Numbers.**" You can use the course number for the job number.
2. At the end of each day, make a Daily To Do list for the following day
3. Add items each day as needed.
4. Track your time by each job number during the day using the **To Do List & Time Tracking** method described on p. 109.

How to Use the
To Do List & Time Tracking

Agency compensation models have changed considerably from the days when ad placement commissions were the primary source of the agency's compensation, to now encompassing a wide variety of compensation models. While there are differences between project-based work , fee-based agency of record agreements, and pay-for-performance, it is still true that most people, both account and creative, will need to account for their time by job number.

It is therefore essential that Creatives always require a job number before beginning new work. While an occasional emergency does happen in which work needs to start before a job number has been issued (although this is more usually reflective of people ignoring agency procedures), this should be the exception rather than the rule.

Many people work on too many jobs during each day to be able to precisely recall at the end of the week how they spent their time on Monday.

It is therefore essential that everyone accurately account for their time.

Unfortunately, too many employees of a company get to the end of their work week and have to reconstruct their daily time spent by job number. This is at best an approximation, and at worst is pure fiction.

My practice has been to keep both a list of active job numbers for accounts on which I am working and a daily To Do list on separate pages of a legal pad. Creating the next day's To Do list is the last thing I do each day.

On this daily To Do list I also list the job numbers of accounts I am currently working on, in a box on the right side of the page. As the day proceeds I can make a notation by the job number as I spend time on that account. This mechanism facilitates record keeping even when I am switching between accounts during the day.

To Do: day, date

job #	hrs
12345	2.25
67890	1.50
54321	2.00
98765	3.25

1. first priority
2. second priority
3. third priority
4. fourth item
5. fifth item
6. additional item
   added during
   the day
7. additional item
   added during
   the day

job numbers - client - description

12345	ABC Inc.	storyboard
67890	Acme Corp.	concepts
54321	Scheckyco	concepts
98765	Maestra	planning
23456	Aethel	strategy
23680	Aethel	catalog layout
34567	Midairco	speech
36543	Midairco	identity design

VI. The BAFFLE THEM WITH BS Problem

Providing too much of the wrong information.

"Great!" said George, reviewing the creative work. "But you should replace this with green."

"Um…why?" I asked.

"The client's wife's favorite color is green," replied George.

"As interesting as that may be, you do realize that the client's competition uses green as their signature color?" I asked. "And if we are to build a cohesive brand identity for our client, then we should avoid the color green as a principal brand identity element."

"But the client's wife really, really, likes green."

"The brief specified that the competition uses green," I reminded him.

"But…"

"And the client signed off on the brief, and so did you," I said, as I showed George the brief.

"But, but…the client is always right," said George, with familiar exasperation.

"The client is always the client," I said. "But we're the professionals, and it is our ethical responsibility to give our clients the benefit of our best judgment and expertise, especially when they don't know any better."

The work ended up being green.

Another old saying, this one attributed to W. C. Fields, is "if you can't dazzle them with brilliance, baffle them with BS."

The flip side of **The FORTUNE TELLER Problem** of being provided with insufficient information is when the Creative Team is provided with too much of the wrong type of information.

While creative solution insights can come from unexpected sources of information, irrelevant information can include the client's wife's favorite color, the name of the client's pet poodle, or other information that falls under the general heading of personal taste.

An effective solution is not about what the client merely likes, but about what will work to solve the client's need. This distinction can be made more difficult when the A2C brief is full of client "likes" rather than including the relevant information.

For one type of A2C brief, see pp. 126–127.

See also **The ARTISTE Problem**, p. 156, during the C2A briefing

What is wrong with my
Creative Brief?

Not enough of the right information (that which is relevant).

Too much of the wrong information (that which is irrelevant).

Not complete.

These are a few of the most common problems of some Creative Briefs.

The brief is not paperwork for its own sake, but rather an essential part of the creative process.

The research that goes into the drafting of the brief must lead to actionable insights about the target audience. If the brief doesn't accomplish that essential goal, the brief might as well not be used at all.

The Solution:
Look through each Creative Brief to separate the relevant from the irrelevant information.

If there is relevant information missing, request the missing information.

You should always be looking for clues to the most important insights into the motivations of the target audience described in the brief. A clear description of the target audience (see pp. 50-51 and pp. 126-127), is an absolutely essential piece of an effective Creative Brief.

The Red Herrings Exercise:

1. As a group, draft a Creative Brief for a campaign. Include irrelevant red herrings* in your brief, along with relevant information and insights.

2. Exchange your brief with another group.

3. Work together to identify both the red herrings and the important insights.

4. Present your findings to the class.

* A **red herring** *is a distraction from what is relevant or important, and can lead to an incorrect conclusion.*

VII. The I'M NOT YOUR SLACKER FRIEND Problem

Setting a fake deadline

One Monday morning Jack the account executive entered my office. "The client liked it," he announced. "They want it Friday."

I laughed. "Good one, Jack."

Jack wasn't laughing. "I'm serious," he said.

"Jack," I began. "I told you that this complex project has to be produced by multiple vendors, and then assembled, and will take five WEEKS. Not five days."

"If you pull out all the stops, how soon can this be delivered?" asked Jack.

"Five weeks," I answered.

"What if you call in favors from vendors, and have people work overtime?" he asked.

"Five weeks," I replied. "Jack, I'm good, but even I can't change the laws of physics. Materials have to be ordered and shipped. Items manufactured and printed. It will take five weeks."

"Well," grumbled Jack. "Do what you can."

Five weeks later:
"Here you go, Jack. You can tell the client that you are on the way."

"Oh, the client is on vacation. He just wanted to be sure it would be done when he gets back."

We've all known that guy. The slacker friend who always shows up late. Maybe his friends start telling him to show up at 5 when they actually want him there at 6. His friends start lying to him about the real time he is to arrive.

Creatives are not that guy.

The first rule I teach design, marketing, and advertising students is "Never, Ever Miss a Deadline."

But the second rule I teach them is "Be as certain as possible before you agree to a deadline, that the deadline is real."

A deadline may be dictated by a client, or based on other external factors such as the dates of a trade show or the production schedule of a magazine. Deadlines may also be based on the actual length of time that all the steps of the creative process will take.

A "real" deadline is one that accounts for immutable external factors and is agreed to by all stakeholders before a delivery date is promised to a client.

A "fake" deadline is one that does not account for immutable externals, or is developed in isolation by the Account Team without input from the rest of the agency.

Creatives have to balance many projects in different stages of completion at the same time, including the contributions of many people who are also juggling several projects. A false deadline throws that careful schedule planning off, and is disrespectful of the professionalism of Creatives.

Production Timeline

A production timeline that defines deadlines, including the dates for the completion of intermediate steps, is essential for an agency or a freelancer. It is also a valuable tool for students.

When you plan your time in advance, you are more able to avoid the last-minute crunch of getting a project completed to turn in on time. You are also able to have more time to refine your work including proofreading and finalizing precise design details. You will also be able to accommodate the unexpected changes and client requests that inevitably occur along the way.

If work is built on a solid foundation of research, ideation, critical thinking, and analysis, this refinement can elevate the work from "good enough" to excellent, from a merely passing grade to an outstanding one.

In short, better time planning is one tool for getting better grades. It's not a guarantee, but not planning is pretty certain to keep you from achieving the best work of which you are capable. And really, why would you want to do anything less than your best?

The Solution:

Provide real deadlines. Work with the Creative Team to develop a production timeline.

Don't promise a delivery date to the client until you check with the Creative Team.

The Production Timeline Exercise:

1. By the end of the first week of your semester, create a production timeline for all your classes, due dates, and work obligations. See the instructions in the resource on pp. 128–129.

2. Keep track of how closely you are able to adhere to your timeline schedule. Note how much longer it took to do certain tasks, and how much more quickly you were able to accomplish others.

VIII. The UNPRICED ITEMS Problem

Not capturing all costs in the Start of Work Agreement

"Does your budget include a stylist?" asked Marc the client.

"Of course," replied Rick, my boss and the owner of the agency.

We wrapped up our meeting.

As we were walking to our car, Rick turned to me and asked, "What's a stylist?"

I stopped, and turned to look at him.

"A stylist is the person who takes care of the makeup and hair, and clothing prep for the models during the photo shoot," I explained. "You mean you didn't include the stylist in the budget?"

"I guess not," admitted Rick. "Is there any way to do without a stylist?"

"No. The client is going to be there throughout the shoot," I answered. "And the stylist is a critical part of the team if we are to have quality results."

"Can't you do it?" asked Rick.

"I'm the art director, and I'll be busy art directing," I answered.

"What's the cost of a stylist?" asked Rick.

"The same as it was three days ago..." I answered, "...in the info I gave you about the costs of the photo shoot."

Along with the A2C Creative Brief, another important document — the **Start of Work Agreement** — is a detailed description of the of work to be undertaken by the agency.

This document clearly describes all the elements in a project that have an associated cost for creation, development, production, and administration.

This description of what the agency will provide for the fees they are charging is often referred to as the **Scope of Work.**

When the Start of Work Agreement defining the extent (scope) of the work for which the agency will be compensated is incomplete due to errors by the Account Team or Creative Team, any additional costs will be borne by the agency.

Creating a useful
Start of Work Agreement

The essential element of a functional, useful Start of Work Agreement include:
1. *The schedule, including intermediate and final deadlines*
2. *The deliverables*
3. *The budget and payment schedule*
4. *Who has the authority to approve the work the agency delivers*
5. *The date the agreement is signed*
6. *Signatures of the parties with authority to approve the agreement*

The deliverables define the scope of the work so that any additional deliverable requested will fall outside the scope and require a Project Change Notification (PCN).

A Start of Work Agreement is also essential for freelancers. While an agency may expect that a client will pay after 30 or even 90 days, freelancers often request sooner partial payments. For example, 1/2 + 1/2 means that 50% of the agreed fee is paid at the start of work, with the balance paid after the work is delivered. 1/3 + 1/3 + 1/3 means that the fee is paid in equal thirds at the beginning, middle, and end of the job.

A particularly useful technique for freelancers is to describe phases in the Start of Work. For example, the first phase could include research, planning, and concepting. The second phase could include writing and design. The third phase could include production, implementation, and delivery.

The Solution:

After the client hires your agency for an account or a specific project, draft a Start of Work Agreement to make certain that all parties are literally on the same page about the **Scope of Work** that the client is buying.

The Start of Work Exercise:

When you are assigned a group project, follow these steps:

1. As a group, develop a complete list of steps required to accomplish the project successfully.
2. As a group, agree who will work on each step.
3. Write up these steps and assignments as a Start of Work Agreement, and have the group members sign the agreement.
4. As the project progresses, create a PCN for any unanticipated additional steps that need to be accomplished.
5. At the end of the project, each member of the team should evaluate how successful each person was in completing their assigned tasks.
6. Submit this peer evaluation to your instructor, so that the credit for the project can be accurately determined.

IX. The SLIPPERY SLOPE Problem

Allowing scope creep to damage the profit, schedule, or quality of the work

"Are you busy?" asked Louie the account manager, while knocking on my office door.

"Always," I replied with a smile. "How can I help you?"

"This is for that thing you are working on," said Louie, handing me a memo.

I glanced at the memo.

"This appears to be a request for additional work on the project," I stated.

"If you can just do that, the client would appreciate it a lot," explained Louie.

"If you can just wait until I estimate the time and costs for this additional work, then get the client's signature approving the PCN that Jim (the account executive) will issue, I can get right on this," I said.

"I had a feeling you were going to say that," said Louie glumly.

Even when the **Start of Work Agreement** (see p. 114, The UNPRICED ITEMS Problem), which defines the extent of the work for which the agency will be compensated, is complete and detailed, clients will often ask for additional services that were not described in the document. These services are outside the Scope of the Work, or simply "**out of scope.**"

When the agency accepts these requests without charging additional fees, this is commonly referred to as **Scope Creep.**

These additional services can, and generally should, incur additional fees paid to the agency. The Account Team should notify the client when such requests are out of scope, and that the agency will be issuing a document describing the additional services and associated fees. This notification document is sometimes referred to as a **Project Change Notification (PCN)**, but goes by many names.

The Account Team understandably wants to please their clients, correctly believing that a happy client is more likely to be a repeat customer.

However, when the Account Team agrees to do work outside the agreed scope, this causes four potential, serious problems.

The first problem is that the agency, usually the Creative Team, is committing to do work for which the agency is not being compensated. This is a loss of profitability for the agency.

A second, related problem is that the clients become conditioned to getting extra work for free. This increases the likelihood that such free work will become the expected norm.

The third problem of Scope Creep is that critical deadlines, for this client or others, can be missed, since the Creative Team is burdened by working on items not in the original production schedule. This limits the success of other projects, and also limits the ability of the agency to accept new work.

The fourth problem is that the project may fail entirely. When more work is requested but the timeframe is not increased, the negative consequences can include poor quality control, poor integration of the new elements, and ultimately a less than entirely successful project.

Such a failure can damage the agency's reputation and relationship with the client. This can have a lasting negative effect on the agency's success.

The Solution:
Make certain that the Start of Work Agreement (see pp. 105 and 115) is complete before it is signed. Include a disclaimer in the Start of Work Agreement about additional work incurring costs.

If you receive a request for additional work not covered by the Start of Work Agreement, check with your supervisor and the Account Team. Although you may have to estimate additional hours and costs, it is the Account Team's responsibility to issue a PCN.

The Time Estimation Exercise:
As you work on your own projects, compare the actual time you spend to your estimate of time in your Planning Timeline (see pp. 128–129). If you spend more time than you expected, is it because you underestimated the time needed, or because you added additional work to the original project specifications?

X. The CRUSH DURING KICKOFF Problem

Falling in love with your first idea

Even as we sat in the briefing meeting, I could see Evan's excitement building.

"I've got it!" he said to me as we left the conference room.

"Got what, exactly?" I asked him.

"The killer idea for this campaign!"

"That's great," I said. "But we haven't thoroughly examined the situation, the target audience, and the client's own presumptions about their problems."

"Yeah, I know all that," replied Evan. "But this idea is so kick-ass!"

"Great!" I said, with convincingly feigned enthusiasm. "Write it down, sketch it out, get it onto paper where you won't forget it. Then we can evaluate your killer idea properly."

"Thanks," said Evan, encouraged.

"Of course," I continued, "you are certainly going to come up with a bunch of other ideas too, after you get more info on the client's situation."

"What? Oh....of course. Plenty more where this came from!"

"Excellent! Let's convene later to see what insights we can gather from the client's information."

Creatives have a lot of ideas. That's a good attribute.

But one of the problems is that the first idea may seem like the best, truest, and only idea.

That's because creatives often harbor the secret fear that THEY WILL NEVER, EVER HAVE ANOTHER GOOD IDEA AGAIN!

Like most fears, this one is not rational IF the Creatives have mastered the **Creative Process** (see Chapter 5) rather than simply relying on the nebulous concept of inspiration.

Creatives study and train to learn more than technical skills. They study the process of creation. Following a repeatable process enables Creatives to produce effective work even when they are not "inspired."

Anyone can have one good idea. A well-trained, experienced Creative will have one great idea after another. Their creativity is repeatable.

A useful tool that Creatives use to come up with new ideas and to develop their ideas in new ways is **Osborn's Checklist** (see p. 80–81).

See also The FIRE, READY, AIM Problem, p. 144, which can occur during the Creative Team to Account Team (C2A) briefing.

Parking Lots in note taking

When I am taking notes during a meeting, I frequently have ideas about possible solutions or about other situations, projects, or problems. Rather than get stuck on these ideas and neglect the content of the ongoing meeting, or worse yet forget about my idea entirely, I use a Parking Lot.

Similar to the practice of a Parking Lot board during a Brainstorm, where ideas with potential that are off topic or out of sequence are placed so as not to be forgotten, I use the same idea on my own notes.

I keep my meeting notes on the left side of the page, and reserve the right side of the page for a series of Parking Lots. When an idea I want to capture and return to later occurs to me, I write and/or sketch this on the right side of the page and draw a box around it. ➔➔➔➔➔➔➔

In that way I have captured the idea for potential later use.

Meeting Notes
date, time, place

Notes:

① Parking
Lot note

② Parking
Lot note

③ Parking
Lot note

The Solution:

I always capture my first ideas on paper, even during a kickoff meeting (see **Parking Lots** above). In doing so, I keep from getting stuck on that idea, and can proceed to develop other solutions.

Ignoring your first idea is similar to ignoring your feelings. They have a way of reasserting themselves at inopportune times. Just as in an emotionally difficult situation, avoidance is not a good practice. The best way forward is through. Deal with the idea so that you can move on to the next, and possibly better solution.

The Parking Lot Exercise:

1. During your next meeting or lecture, use the **Parking Lot** note-taking idea described in the Sidebar above on this page.

2. After your meeting or lecture, capture your Parked ideas into a digital format.

3. Evaluate your Parked ideas, and develop them further if warranted. Ideas on other problems or subjects can be sorted into files for those topics.

XI. The QUESTION RELUCTANCE Problem

Not asking relevant questions

It was the first day for Suzy, our new intern. I had seen her impressive digital portfolio of student work.

"I'm glad you're here!" I said welcomingly. "I have some work for you to do."

I showed her to the mat room. "Here are hard copies of the layouts. Here are mounting boards, X-ACTO® knives and blades, the spray booth and supplies, and the adhesive roller," I explained as I showed her where to find all the needed supplies.

"Trim, layout, and mount each set of printouts on a board. Let me know if you need anything," I said. "I'll check on you later."

After a while, having reached a break point in my own work, and not having seen or heard anything of Suzy, I returned to the mat room.

I saw Suzy with bandages on almost every finger, and a mess of paper and supplies.

"Uh...How's it going?" I asked.

"I...I've had....had a few p...p...problems," said Suzy, choking back tears.

I looked a the mounting boards. Every thing was crooked, every board had ragged edges, and there were smudges of glue everywhere.

"Well," I began, "this won't really work for what we need. But we can do this over."

At this point Suzy's tears began in earnest. I handed her a tissue.

"Tell me," I asked. "Has anyone ever shown you how to use the tools in a mat room?"

Suzy sniffled, shook her head, and wiped away tears.

"I'm sorry for assuming that you had. All you had to do is ask. I'm happy to show you how to use the mat room without hurting yourself," I said, reassuringly. "Shall we get started?"

Suzy nodded.

"Great!" I then demonstrated the proper use of the supplies, tools, and materials, while thinking that every designer needs to learn to use an X-ACTO® knife without hurting themselves.

Students are often reluctant to ask questions in the classroom.[3]

Sometimes this reluctance is from shyness, or language problems, or thinking that they should already know the answer.

This **Question Reluctance** is a problem in the classroom, as it hampers the instructor's ability to help students master the material.

In a professional setting, Question Reluctance can derail the process of creating effective solutions for clients.

This is true whether the reluctance is on the part of the Account Team or the Creative Team.

Prepared Questions
for meetings

You should come to any meeting with a list of questions you have prepared in advance. Whether the meeting is within a company, with a client, or a classroom meeting, your preparation contributes to your success.

For a project kickoff meeting, questions are often prepared in response to the Creative Brief (see the sample brief on pp. 126–127).

It is often useful to ask for clarification of information in the brief. It can also be necessary to ask additional questions regarding insights into the client's customers, if that topic was not adequately covered in the brief. What do their customers think, and how do they feel, about the client's brand and their interactions with the company?

Other types of meetings require the preparation of questions relevant to the subjects of those meetings.

Fundamental to being able to ask relevant, insightful questions, whether in a client meeting or a classroom, is reading the provided or assigned material in advance. It is always obvious when a person has not read the material in advance, and is attempting to bluff their way through a meeting or class.

The Solution:

Have a prepared list of questions for specific types of meetings, including client meetings, kickoff meetings, update meetings, or **project "post mortem"** meetings (which review the effectiveness of the project process and outcomes).

During the meeting, see if your questions are answered. If so, you can simply note the answer. However, you may find that the answer to one question causes other questions to arise.

If your prepared questions are not answered, or you have follow-up questions, you should ask them at the appropriate time in the meeting.

The Prepared Questions Exercise:

For each assigned reading, develop a list of:
1. Statements you don't understand, and that you can ask for clarification on during class.
2. Anything about which the accuracy seems questionable, or for which the author has not cited a credible source, or proven to your satisfaction.
3. Anything you disagree with. However, you should research the subject and provide a source to support your contradictory view.

The A2C Briefing Solutions

Four Account and Four Creative Steps to Enable Creative Excellence

In this chapter I have described the many problems that can occur during the A2C briefing. But fortunately the solutions presented for these problems have been proven to work.

It is not enough, however, to simply read these solutions. Implementing a process change in an organization is difficult. Change requires understanding and a commitment not only from the organization's management, but also from the employees who will be the people implementing the changes.

Without such a commitment, people will fall back on old habits, and the problems will remain.

Of course, organizational improvement is an ongoing process. As circumstances change, so must organizations. Undoubtedly, new problems will arise with any change. But the solutions summarized below can continue to work.

Account Team:
FOUR STEPS TO SUCCESS During the A2C Briefing

A summary of the solutions to Account Team A2C problems

Each of the separate problems described also has a particular solution applicable to that problem. However, the practices described below will work together to help prevent the problems from occurring.

These are the means by which the Account Team could help the Creative Team excel, and thereby improve the chances of the Account Team's success in the eyes of their clients.

1. **Provide the right information**
   What Creatives really need from a briefing is the right information about the situation, the company, the competition, the competitive marketing, and the target audiences. Provide this information, but don't dictate the solutions. Don't dictate the medium. Do define what success will look like at the end of the project or campaign.

2. **Budget time to explore ideas**
   Listen to the Creatives' ideas. Encourage their unconventional, uncomfortable, challenging ideas. Push the Creatives to explore newer, edgier, riskier, bigger ideas. It's always easier to pull back from an "out there" idea than it is to push a conventional idea to be more than it is.

3. **Budget time to refine the work**
   While modern technology has increased productivity, it still takes time to think, concept, develop, and evaluate new ideas. Give the Creative Team time to explore ideas and refine the work.

4. **Develop a timeline WITH the Creative Team**
   Respect the Creative Team enough to give them a functional schedule and achievable deadlines (see p. 112). These are usually accomplished by the Account Team and the Creative Team developing a timeline together.

Creative Team:
FOUR STEPS TO SUCCESS During the A2C Briefing

A summary of the solutions to Creative Team A2C problems

The solutions for each of the separate problems described does not only fall to the Account Team. These four steps are the means by which the Creative Team can improve the chances of the Account Team's success with their clients, and the likelihood of successful outcomes for the campaign.

1. **Ask the right questions**

    To help the Account Team provide the right information, the Creative Team needs to be prepared to ask the right questions. This requires reading the available information in advance of the briefing, and developing a list of relevant questions.

    Just as in the exercise for The QUESTION RELUCTANCE Problem, p. 121, following a careful reading of the advance information, the Creative Team should develop a list of clarifying questions and challenges to unsupported assumptions made in the brief.

    The Creative Team should research the subject and provide sources to support any contradictory view.

2. **Learn to accurately estimate the time you need**

    The skill of accurate time estimation is challenging to develop. Like any difficult, advanced skill, practice is essential. Use the time planning and estimation tools described on pp 128–131 to develop the essential ability to accurately estimate the time it will take you to accomplish your best work.

3. Keep working to master the process

The education of a creative professional in any discipline includes training in skills and conceptual thinking. These are essential, but the most important element to master is the creative process.

I was taught that if I "worked the process," then the product I wanted would result, but if I focused on the end result, I would be less likely to achieve it. Over the years this has proven to be true.

4. Give them what they ask for, but ALSO give them what they need

Respect the challenges facing the Account Team enough to give them what they are asking for. But also respect your own knowledge and abilities enough to exceed the expectations by going beyond the requirements to create more effective solutions.

The Essential A2C CREATIVE BRIEF

Every agency has their own unique version of a Creative Brief. However, the objective of the brief is always to provide essential insights that enable the creation of effective solutions by the Creative Team. This is one version of a brief.

THE INFO
Describes the client and the audience

WHO..
1. **...is the client?**

WHAT...
2. **... is their history and background?**

3. **... is the brand positioning?**
    - What is our client's stand (goals, beliefs, aspirations) to our target audience?
    - How does our client see itself?
    - What themes, slogans, buzzwords, images, or corporate goals are used by our client?
    - What themes, slogans, buzzwords, or images are to be avoided?

4. **... is the product/service positioning?**
    - What are the product/service promises?

5. **... is the current relationship of the brand and the product with the target audience?**
    - Is there an existing relationship?
    - What are the strengths of the current relationship?
    - What are the weaknesses, current or past objections or brand liabilities to overcome?

6. **... is the client's Unique Value Proposition?**
    - What is the unique contribution the client's company, product and services provide to their market, different from their competitors?

WHO...
7. **... is the target audience?**
    - Audience Type (Examples: dealership principal, salesperson, sales manager, consumers, buyer)
    - What is the demographic profile of the target audience?
      - Age range
      - % Male/Female
      - % Married
      - Household income
      - % with children
      - % college
      - Occupation category
      - Other relevant data
    - Psychographic information (Example: decision makers; influencer; assertive; early-adopter)

8. **... is the client's competition?**

THE OPPORTUNITY
Describes the situation and the objectives

WHAT...

9. ... problem are we being asked to solve?
- What is the client's stated objective?
- What is the deeper objective or problem that is the cause of the stated objective?

10. ...are the unrealized opportunities?
- What can be redefined or done differently to change the limitations of how the brand is viewed?

HOW...

11. ...will we define success?
- How will we recognize that we have succeeded?

12. ...will we measure success?
- How will we collect data before and after the program/campaign/project? (How we measure success depends how we define success.)

THE INSIGHTS
Describes target audience's motivations, needs, wants, and decision-making processes

WHAT...

13. ...do consumers want?
...do consumers feel?
...do consumers think?
- In the situations where they need or use a product or service, what are their needs, wants, and desires?
- What level of Maslow's Hierarchy of Needs are we addressing?

WHAT...

14. ... is the main thought we want to communicate?
- If we can only express one clear point to the target, what would engage them quickly and compel them to take the desired action?

15. ... means do we have to substantiate that one clear thought?
- What proof can we provide (documentation, statistics, focus group results, etc.)?

WHAT

16. ...are we trying to motivate the target audience to think, to feel, to do?

17. ... tone of voice is appropriate?
- Knowing the target audience enables us to form a voice that is in sync with theirs, a voice that helps connect with the target. Is it the tone of a friend, casual and conversational? Is it the tone of a nurturer or confidante? Is it urgent and time sensitive, or businesslike and to the point?

18. ... is the call to action?
- What response mechanism enables the target audience to take the desired action to meet the objectives?

The PRODUCTION PLANNING TIMELINE

How to create and use a calendar to avoid the last-minute crunch

Students have a unique problem and opportunity with regard to their schedules.

Unlike people who can go home at the end of their work day and forget about work until tomorrow, students always have more to do. There is always more reading, research, studying, or review. Even when homework is project based, there is more ideation and refinement possible. This situation presents a scheduling problem that often leads to last minute cramming for exams and all-night study sessions.

But this situation also presents an opportunity. In many work situations, project deadlines and requirements often change (see **The SLIPPERY**

SLOPE Problem, p. 118), and new projects on short deadlines are inserted into existing schedules. Students have an opportunity to set a schedule for a semester that can be adhered to more closely, although not without flexibility.

By the end of the first week of every semester, students should have all the syllabi for their classes. These syllabi will have due dates for every exam and project. These due dates can form the basis of a production planning timeline. The use of such a timeline will help identify the available hours during which studying and assignments can be accomplished.

Steps to creating a production planning timeline:

1. Create a four-month calendar (see one month example on the next page)
2. Block out the times of class meetings (shown in gray)
3. Block out travel time to and from class (shown in gray)
4. Block out any other commitments, including work and athletics (shown in gray)
5. Block out time for meals (shown in white)
6. See how much open time you have left on the schedule. (shown in black)
7. At the end of the first week of the semester, use the syllabi from all your classes to make a list of all the assignments due in each class, including readings, papers, and projects.
8. Identify the due dates of all assignments, presentations, and the dates of all exams
9. Put these due dates on the calendar when they are to occur.
10. Now estimate how much time it will take to accomplish each assignment. (see **Time Estimation and Pricing** on page 132).
11. For each assignment, set intermediate deadlines for yourself.
12. Block out reading and study time for specific classes from the available open time left on the schedule.
13. Any time left, if any, can be used for sleep.

TIME MANAGEMENT PLANNING CALENDAR

	Week 1						
	M	Tu	W	Th	F	Sa	Su
8		travel		travel			
8:30	1.5 HRS	Class 3	1.5 HRS	Class 3	4 HRS	4 HRS	
9							
9:30							
10	travel	travel	travel	travel			
10:30	Class 1	2 HRS	Class 1	2 HRS			
11							
11:30							
12	travel		travel				
12:30	Lunch	Lunch	Lunch	Lunch	Lunch	Lunch	Lunch
1	1 HR	travel	1 HR	travel	4 HRS	4 HRS	4 HRS
1:30		Class 4		Class 4			
2	travel		travel				
2:30	Class 2		Class 2				
3		travel		travel			
3:30		3 HRS		3 HRS			
4							
4:30							
5	Dinner		Dinner		Dinner	Dinner	Dinner
5:30	travel		travel		travel		
6	Work		Work		Work		
6:30		Dinner		Dinner			
7		4 HRS		4 HRS			4 HRS
7:30							
8							
8:30							
9	travel		travel		travel		
9:30							
10							
10:30							

Example Weekly Totals

in class:	12	*hours*
traveling:	8	*hours*
working:	9	*hours*
available for homework/studying:	50	*hours*

TIME ESTIMATION and PRICING

How to calculate how long it will take, and how much to charge

One of the most frequently asked questions from students in the creative professions is "How much do I charge for freelance work?"

Developing the knowledge and ability to set an appropriate price for freelance work also develops the skill to estimate how long work will take to accomplish.

This latter skill is also needed by employed professionals who must be able to estimate the time it will take them to accomplish their assigned tasks.

Developing this skill is an outgrowth of the time planning and time recording processes described on pp. 113 and 131). By first recording the time actually spent on types of work, an awareness of time is developed. Through practice, you will get better at providing accurate time estimates.

There are four common pricing methods:

The Task Method
This method looks at the time required to accomplish each task, applies an hourly rate to the time, and the total is the price charged for the finished work. The Task Method procedure and example task details are described on the following page.

The Job Method
This method charges a total price for the work, without providing details of the hours required. For creatives just beginning to freelance, the Job Method price presented to the client is actually based on the total derived by using The Task Method. Even when using The Task Method to calculate a total price to charge the client, a freelancer should never provide their hourly rate to the client. This only encourages clients to negotiate the hourly rate, rather than focusing on the total.

There is an advantage to presenting a job-based total to the client. If the freelancer is able to satisfactorily complete and deliver the job in fewer hours than originally calculated, the freelancer makes more "per hour." However, the corresponding disadvantage is that if the job takes longer than estimated, the freelancer's realized hourly rate is lower.

Also, once a job price is quoted, it is difficult to quote a higher price on subsequent, similar jobs, leading to the exploitation of the new or inexperience freelancer.

The Day-Rate Method
This is commonly used by photographers. Calculating an hourly rate, then multiplying by eight hours equals the day rate a photographer will charge.

Photographers typically charge a minimum of a half-day for any work. The half-day rate is typically for five hours at the eight hour rate.
- Hourly rate x 8 hours = 1 day
- + expenses
- Still requires estimation of time to create work, meetings, all revisions, etc.
- Never give your hourly rate
- Minimum 1/2 day = 5 hours

The Double Employee Rate Method
This is a rule-of-thumb method, in which the freelancer charges double the hourly rate of an agency employee, because the freelancer needs to cover health care costs, retirement savings, and other expenses not charged directly to the client.

The Task Method

Procedure:
1. Write down each task, in detail, in order
2. Break tasks into smallest units
3. Estimate hours necessary for each task unit
4. Figure an hourly rate for your calculations (never give your hourly rate to client)
5. Multiply hours needed x rate = cost of task
6. Multiply task cost by "**degree of difficulty multiplier**" ➜
7. Ask yourself if job is worth doing for what you can charge.

Examples of Task Details:
1. Travel to and from client meeting
2. Meeting time
3. Write up notes
4. Email notes
5. Planning and timeline development
6. Research outside costs
7. Write quote
8. Modify quote as needed
9. Competitive research
10. Write up research notes
11. Write creative brief
12. Thumbnail concepts
13. Present concepts
14. Design and copy development
15. Prepare presentation
16. Schedule meeting, in person or online
17. Meeting time (plus travel if needed)
18. Write up meeting notes
19. Design and copy modification
20. Schedule meeting, in person or online
21. Meeting time (plus travel if needed)
22. Make final changes
23. Present final work
24. Delivery/implementation
25. Invoice client
26. Archive files

The Degree of Difficulty Multiplier

This is similar to how the scores in a diving competition are calculated. In those competitions, the quality of the dive execution is multiplied by the degree of difficulty of the dive attempted. The result is the total score awarded.

Similarly the Degree of Difficulty Multiplier is used when the client and/or any intermediary person (account executive, account manager, project manager, direct client contact, etc.) is difficult to work with, and complicates the process by their involvement.

While the hours required to complete a complex project can be calculated, the Degree of Difficulty Multiplier acounts for the intangilble complications introduced by other people involved in the process.

A multiplier may be 1.5 or more (I worked with a colleague who I assigned a multiplier of x5!). However, you should not tell the person you assign a multiplier that you have done so.

Once the Task Method total is calculated, the Degree of Difficulty Multiplier is applied to arrive at the total price charged for the job.

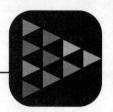

PUTTING the PIECES TOGETHER

*Using the Start of Work Agreement + The Production Planning Timeline +
The Daily To Do List + The Creative Brief + Work Orders*

The tools and methods described in this chapter and others do not exist in isolation, but rather work in the correct order and combination to build the oppotunity to create excellent work.

As illustrated in the diagram on the following page, the process begins with a Start of Work Agreement (see pp. 114–115).

Within the Start of Work Agreement should be a list of deliverables.

This list of deliverables should be developed into a clear Production Schedule using the Time Estimation and Production Planning tools on pp. 128–131.

Finally, the Production Schedule is broken down into a Daily To Do list (see p. 109), in order to keep the project on track for on-time delivery and within budget.

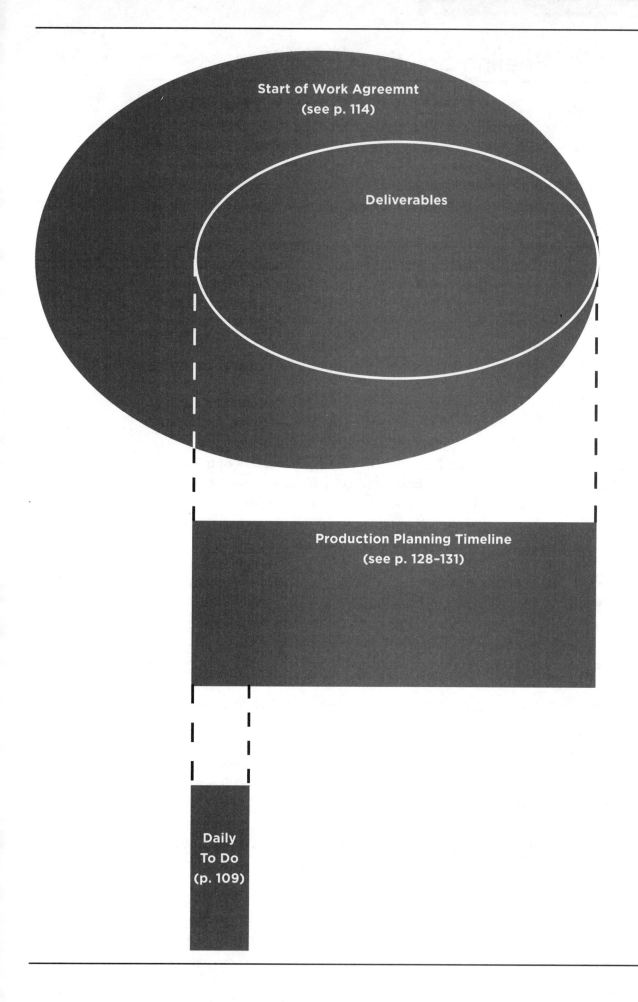

Start of Work Agreemnt
(see p. 114)

Deliverables

Production Planning Timeline
(see p. 128-131)

Daily
To Do
(p. 109)

The A2C Briefing Solutions Exercises

Exercise 1: The Everyday Idea Book

An **idea book** is a small, easily carried, book for recording ideas, observations, inspirations, sketches, and notes.

The old saying (attributed to a Qing Dynasty work) "The faintest ink is better than the best memory" was the inspiration for my habit of always carrying an idea book. Most people have had the unfortunate experience of thinking of a great idea or solution to a problem, then being unable to recall the specifics later. Hence the value of writing it down for later use.

I call it an idea book rather than a sketch book, because it is useful for everyone, including people who don't regularly sketch

The idea book can be blank, ruled, gridded, or some combination of these. It can be softbound or hardbound, pocket sized or carried in a day bag. Even if your preference is for a larger idea book to carry in a bag, I recommend also having a pocket-size idea book for carrying when a day bag is too cumbersome.

1. Write the name of every class or project on which you are working at the top of a two-page spread in your idea book.

2. Set the goal of adding at least one new idea, inspiration, reference, thought, or note to each spread each day.

3. Transfer items from each spread to your Process Book (see p. 180) every couple of days.

4. Keep your idea book on your night stand. Record your ideas before you go to sleep. Upon waking, you can also record your dreams on pages set aside for that purpose.

5. After a few weeks, take note of when ideas occur to you. Is it during the day? At night? Upon waking? When doing other tasks?

Exercise 2: Putting the Pieces Together

Beginning with the Creative Brief on pp. 126–127, and referring to the process steps and diagram on p. 132–133, and the related resources on pp. 128–131, put all these tools to work on a group project.

1. Begin with drafting a Creative Brief. This requires research and collaboration.

2. Once the group has approved the Creative Brief, draft a Start of Work Agreement. Include all the deliverables that the group must produce.

3. Brainstorm solutions, then evaluate those solutions and choose a direction for the project.

4. Set individual tasks and responsibilities.

5. Work together to estimate how long it will take to accomplish each step of the project.

6. Working back from the due date, develop the production schedule for the overall project.

7. Include coordination meetings in your project production schedule.

8. Include time to revise each person's contribution so that the voice and look of the entire project are consistent.

9. Each person should individually develop a task production schedule for their assigned tasks.

10. Each person should also track the amount of time it actually takes to accomplish a task, then compare this to the estimate. Refer to the To Do LIst & Time Tracking on p. 109.

11. Once the work is completed, meet to review how the process could be improved. Take notes, and apply these improvements to your next team projects and individual projects.

Chapter Notes

1. Maslow, Abraham H. (1969). *Psychology of Science: A Reconnaissance.* Washington D.C.: Gateway Editions, p. 150.

2. Kaplan, Abraham. (1964). *The Conduct of Inquiry: Methodology for Behavioral Science.* San Francisco: Chandler Publishing Co., p. 280.

3. Sparks, Sarah D. (2014). *Students' Help-Seeking Strategies Offer Clues for Educators.* Retrieved from http://www.edweek.org/ew/articles/2014/08/20/01help.h34.html

Chapter 8

Creative Team:
How to Create Your Most Effective
Work and Sell It to the Account Team

*The Twelve Creative Team + Three Account Team Mistakes That Can
Happen During the Creative Briefing (C2A) and How To Fix Them*

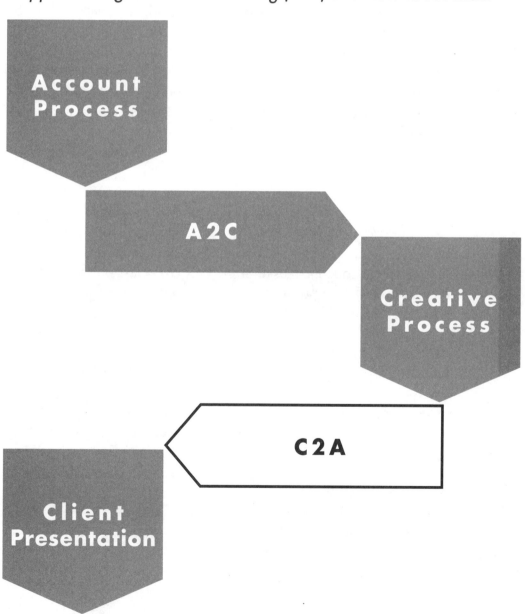

Introduction: The CREATIVES ARE JUST TOO "CREATIVE" Problems

What goes wrong before, during, and after the Creative Briefing (C2A)

Shortly after getting final client signoff on the auto manufacturer's direct mail piece, Tommy the art director left the agency. So I ended up accompanying Jim the print producer to the out-of-town press check.

Our flight arrived and Marv the printing company rep drove us to the plant for the press check. We assumed that this would be a quick, one-day approval trip. After all, the client had approved the final design comps.

When we arrived at the printing plant, the web press was already up to speed, and the first sheets were ready for review.

"Jim," I said, "this doesn't match the client-approved final comps."

"What?" said Jim and Marv in unison.

"Tommy must have changed the files after final client approval. The background is now black, not white. And on this uncoated paper, the black background became washed out and the vehicles look terrible. The client would never approve this."

Jim and Marv just stared at me, then at the comps in my hand, then proof sheets, and then back at me.

"Even if we changed the black to a rich black background in order to alleviate the washed-out black," I continued, "that would only emphasize the poor reproduction of the vehicles."

"I can't sign off on this," I stated firmly. Jim, Marv, and I considered our options. We decided to order a roll of coated paper stock to replace the uncoated paper. That meant we would have to return the following week for a second press check.

When we returned, the printed sheets on the new paper, with the rich black background, looked great.

"Um," began Marv hesitantly, "we are having a problem getting our inline perforation to work. We keep snapping the web, and we're not sure why."

After much deliberation between Marv, his boss, the pressmen, and the press manufacturer's rep, they concluded that the harder coated paper required more pressure to perforate, and the increased pressure was snapping the web. Using less pressure resulted in the paper not successfully perforating.

Eventually, the printed sheets were sent out to a offline perforating operation, then sent back to the web press for folding and final assembly.

Tommy's "small" creative change increased the costs of production and printing, travel and lodging expenses, and caused the project to miss the client's deadline by a month.

The notion that many people have that the practice of art is simply about self expression is a relatively new idea. For many years, what we now think of as fine art was created on commission, with specifications about dimensions, materials, and subject matter written into a contract.

It is understandable that the general public has this mistaken notion of art, unfortunately reinforced by unflattering depictions in film of tempermental, angst-filled artists.

Designers have no such excuse. The problem solving process used in the design disciplines, and the essentially collaborative nature of advertising and marketing communications creation, requires both creativity and functionality. Creativity in advertising is frequently defined as a solution that is both original and useful.

When the Creatives are viewed as being "too creative" it is usually because they didn't follow the creative and collaborative processes.

The relative cost of revisions at different stages of creative development and production

When the Creative Team, the Account Team, or the client make changes during the course of a project, there is always a cost for doing so.

The graphic shown here illustrates the relative cost increase of making changes at various stages of a print project. While this **10X Rule** is more of a rule-of-thumb than a numerically specific calculation, I have found this formula useful to motivate all participants to carefully consider the implications of changes.

Getting the creative right at each stage of the process lessens the likelihood of changes at later, more expensive stages.

The 10X Rule describing the increasing relative cost of changes at various stages of creative development and production

$1 concepting
$10 roughs
$100 comps
$1000 finished files
$10,000 or more on press

Introduction: The CREATIVES ARE JUST TOO "CREATIVE" Problems

What goes wrong before, during, and after the Creative Briefing (C2A)

THE CREATIVE TEAM MISTAKES

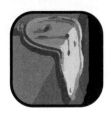

Introduction: The CREATIVES ARE JUST TOO "CREATIVE" Problems

What goes wrong before, during, and after the Creative Briefing (C2A)

THE ACCOUNT TEAM MISTAKES

THE C2A BRIEFING SOLUTIONS

RESOURCES

I. The FIRE, READY, AIM Problem

Sticking with the CRUSH DURING KICKOFF

"Evan, how's it going?" I asked. "What have you got?"

"It's great! This is that really cool idea that I got in the meeting. I've got nearly finished versions for print, and a storyboard. Look at this cool billboard!" Evan was vibrating with excitement.

"This is your first idea? The one that came to you in the kickoff meeting?" I asked.

"Yep. Isn't that cool?"

"Do you have a rationale that explains how this will meet the objectives described in the brief we developed afterward? Is this really a good fit for the target audience and the objectives?" I asked.

"Um, not really. But this is just so cool..."

"You're right. This is a cool, kick-ass idea," I commented. "You've already taken it way further than what is needed for the next go around."

I continued, "What we really need are at least three different concepts that each have the potential to deliver on the objectives defined in the brief."

"So set that idea aside for now, and work up other ideas," I said. "Your first idea can be one of them, IF you can develop a rationale other than it just being a cool idea."

Creatives often stick with their **CRUSH DURING KICKOFF** (see page 118), no matter what additional information they get. I call this the **FIRE, READY, AIM PROBLEM,** because it won't hit the target objectives or audience.

In the context of advertising and marketing, "creative" is a category of problem-solving disciplines. The practitioners of these disciplines follow a specific and repeatable process (see The Creative Process, Chapter 5).

Great ideas are cool, but not just that alone. Really great creative ideas are effective at solving problems.

One of the effects of the **FIRE, READY, AIM PROBLEM** is that a disproportionate amount of time is spent developing an early stage, off-target idea. This eats up the budget early, and doesn't leave sufficient time to develop other ideas to the same level of completion. If such an idea is taken farther into a finished version than other ideas, it will appear to have the endorsement of the agency and could likely be chosen by the client. Oftentimes a slickly presented but ill-conceived idea will be chosen over a better idea that is presented in a less finished form. Of course, the clients should never see any concepts that won't work to solve their needs.

After all, advertising Creative work is not just about how something looks, or how it sounds, or how cool it is. It's about how well it works.

Island of Orphan Ideas

Where do all the Parking Lot ideas go? (see Parking Lots on p. 119).

*I keep both a physical and a digital file folder of ideas that never got used. I call this my **Island of Orphan Ideas.** This is similar to the mental construct of a **Memory Palace,** a visualization tool for sorting and retrieving information from memory.*

Some of these Orphan Ideas were the wrong idea for the situation, but had potential. Some of these were the right solution, but they were never presented to the client. Some of these were great ideas, but the client didn't buy them.

*I keep all of these ideas in addition to my **Folder of Unsent Rants**, where I keep the e-mails and memos I wrote in anger or frustration, but prudently never sent. I revisit my Island of Orphan Ideas for use as thought starters when the occasion warrants.*

You will have to decide the most useful categories for your Island. See the Exercise below on this page.

The Solution:

I always capture my first ideas on paper, even during a kickoff meeting (see **Parking Lots**, p. 119). In doing so, I keep from getting stuck on that idea, and can proceed to develop other solutions.

The Island Exercise

1. With a group of people, discuss categories into which your **Orphan Ideas** can be sorted.

2. Set up a digital folder for your **Island of Orphan Ideas**, and create subfolders for the categories you choose from those you discussed in step 1.

3. File your Orphan ideas into the appropriate digital subfolders.

4. Create a three-ring binder of ideas, notes, and sketches with tabs and hole-punched envelopes that corresponds to the digital categories.

5. Create an index document for your Island. Keep a copy in your digital folder, and a hard copy in the front of your binder.

II. The ROMEO + JULIET Problem

Loving your own ideas too much

"My idea was better before the changes," said Fred as we left the meeting.

"Well, I can understand why you feel that way," I commented. "But you didn't convince anyone in the meeting of that."

Fred continued, "Every detail was there for a reason. I know what I'm doing. I went to school for a reason. I don't understand why they don't recognize a great idea when they see it don't they reallize howsuperbandbrilliantthissouldwi-nawardsandIcouldfinallygetthatfirsttimeofallthe-firstinthewaythatthebetterreasonsloremipsumdo-lorsitametnonsectetur..."

"Should we stop him?" asked Jeff the copywriter, sotto voce.

"Not when he's on a roll like this." I answered quietly. "Let's wait until he has to catch his breath."

Romeo and Juliet is considered to be an example of a great love story. The contrary view is that it was actually about a days-long relationship between two teenagers that resulted in six deaths and lasting misery for their families.

Creatives also fall deeply in love with their other ideas too, and are unwilling to change any part in any way. I call this **The ROMEO AND JULIET Problem**, because it can lead to disaster.

Just as the Montagues and Capulets sabotaged the budding romance, Creatives can sabotage the agreed-upon solution by trying to include some deleted elements from their original idea, or by refusing to accept the changed circumstances of a new solution.

Once the new solution is agreed upon, the Creatives need to bring their energy and expertise to the table, rather than obsessing about the idea that did not move forward.

Creating with a
Creative Rationale

The Creative Rationale is the flip side of the Creative Brief.

While the brief defines the situation for the Creative Team during the C2A briefing, The Creative Rationale describes how the proposed creative execution delivers solutions and will achieve objectives.

That is why a thorough understanding of the A2C Creative Brief is so important, and why a poorly written or incomplete brief will result in an unsatisfactory, ineffective creative solution.

The effective Creative Rationale is built into the creative solution, rather than applied after the fact. Retrofitting a rationale to the creative is never convincing.

See the exercise below on this page. See also "Say This Not That" on page 155.

The Solution:

Every proposed solution should have a **Creative Rationale** (see Creative Rationale sidebar on this page).

But the Creative Rationale should be built in from the beginning, not applied afterwards, and the Creative Rationale has to be in business language, not creative language (see The JARGON PROBLEM, p. 152).

Providing credible sources can enhance the credibility of the Creative Rationale. For example, if certain words, colors, or images can be shown to be preferred by a specific target audience through the citation of a credible study, this can make the rationale more persuasive. This is especially true if the client decision maker is not a member of the target audience.

Exercises:

Begin with an existing Creative Brief. Wherever the brief describes the objectives or problems to be solved, reword those statements to be rationales.

Example:

Creative Brief Objectives	Creative Rationale
Develop product line that appeals to Millennials	Product line name, graphics, colors chosen to appeal to Millennials
Increase trial of new product	Sampling program and incentives will increase trial of new product
Increase repeat purchases	Loyalty program is designed to incentivize repeat purchases

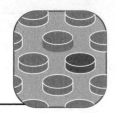

III. The TAKING THE WRONG PRESCRIPTION Problem

A great solution...for a different problem

"We should use a blimp!" proclaimed Betty the enthusiastic copywriter.

"A blimp is cool," she continued. "No one in their business sector has a blimp. It's unique!"

"We can sell the client on using a blimp," said Linda the account executive. "He likes big ideas."

"Great!" added Lewis the art director. "I'll start on designs for the blimp."

"Perfect!" said Linda. "I'll let the client know we'll have something to show him in a few days."

"Excuse me," I interrupted.

Everyone stared at me.

"How will a blimp solve the client's problem?" I asked. "A blimp might make a big impact if we build the advertising around it, and

if we bring in the PR team and we pursue sponsorships and schedule events where the blimp makes sense," I added.

"And as much as I am for a new, big idea," I continued, "what are the cost implications, and how will we calculate the ROI of the blimp?"

"And the press has been savaging the company for recent revelations about expensive executive retreats. A blimp will be perceived as another unnecessary vanity expense."

The room was quiet.

I continued, "blimps ARE cool. But let's look for ways to really solve the most critical problem the client has. Their public image."

In the process of creating solutions, the Creative Team will come up with interesting and unique ideas. However, not all ideas will be effective solutions to the specific problem(s) facing a client. Sometimes an idea is a great solution to a different problem. This is closely related to the problem of prescribing the wrong solution, and so I call this **The TAKING THE WRONG PRESCRIPTION Problem.**

With prescribed or over-the-counter medicines, an effective remedy for one problem will not work for a completely different problem, and may actually exacerbate the symptoms, and prolong the illness.

So it is for creative solutions. The wrong solution could actually make the client's problem worse. As illustrated in the example above, a creative tactic that is perceived as extravagantly expensive will further alienate consumers and stakeholders who are upset about stock price declines or high executive compensation and "golden parachutes" for ousted CEOs.

The Importance of
Aligning
Solutions & Problems

One of the challenges facing Creatives is developing solutions that will achieve specific objectives. In order to create effective solutions, the problems and objectives must be clearly defined. To be clearly defined, an objective must be stated in numerical, measurable terms and have a target date for achieving the objective.

Is the challenge one of increasing sales and profitability in the short term?
Or of increasing the strength of the brand in the longer term?
Is it a matter of increasing awareness among the target audience?
Who is the target audience?
Where is the target audience on the traditional purchase funnel?

Different tactics are most appropriate for moving consumers from a specific stage of the traditional Purchase Funnel to the next. While a pricing reduction or incentive may move someone from consideration into purchase, it takes an awareness building tactic to move people from unaware to aware.

To be effective, a solution must be aligned with the problem or objective.

The Solution:
The Creative Brief should clearly identify the relevant background, competitive situation, and client's strategic challenges. (See Strategy and Tactics, p. 101)

Creative solutions must be evaluated against how well the solution addresses the challenges described in the brief.

Solution Deconstruction Exercise:
In this exercise, you will first identify types of creative solutions, then find business problems that would be solved by those solutions. This backwards approach will make it easier to recall solutions when you encounter problems later. For example:

Types of Creative Solutions ⟶	**Business Problems**
New brand identity/logo design	Consumer perception of company is that it is outdated, stodgy.
Responsive website for product information	Company introduces new products so often that print brochures are quickly outdated.

IV. The SOUL KILLER Problem

Self-censoring your great ideas

"Why bother," he said. "They'll never show it to the client. It will never even get out of the office."

"Fred," I replied, "I understand how you feel. And I don't disagree with you. It is very likely that they won't agree to present this to the client."

"But keep pitching your ideas. Keep thinking of new and better solutions. Either you will convince them you are right, or you will move on with a portfolio of killer ideas."

"Who knows," I continued. "Maybe we can get your idea included in the presentation to the focus group."

Every job has challenges, including tedious tasks, paperwork, and other related obligations. But these necessary ancillary tasks are not what creates a Soul Killing environment.

It is not only possible, but very likely, that you will one day work for someone who repeatedly vetoes what you think of as your most brilliant, inspired ideas. Eventually this leads to self-censorship, where you first don't present those ideas, and then you even stop coming up with them. That is why I call this **The SOUL KILLER Problem**. Because if you let that happen, you go from being a Creative to a hack.

You should understand, however, that if you keep "fighting the good fight," that is, keep pushing the envelope to create more effective, unique, breakthrough solutions, it is possible that rather than changing the work environment, you will become even more frustrated.

When you recognize that this describes your situation, it is time to look for a new job. This is where your great ideas can help.

You should keep copies of all your concepts. Even if, and maybe especially if, your ideas are not chosen, you will still have them for your portfolio. I call these **Unpublished Concepts.** Some of the best work I have created have been unpublished concepts, and are some of the best pieces in my portfolio. This work will show a potential employer what you are capable of when you have a supportive situation in which to work and thrive.

The Solution:
Giving the client what they need is more important for both the long-term success of their business, and the reputation of the agency, than giving the client only what they ask for. But not everyone you work with will understand that. You need to work to convince the naysayers of the value of your ideas.

A portfolio of your best

Unpublished Concepts

Having a place to keep your great ideas helps derail the onset of malaise that can come from working in a Soul Killer environment. By keeping those innovative, effective concepts in a file, with the intention of including them in your portfolio, you can forestall the danger of becoming a self-censoring Creative.

When you do include your great unsold ideas in your portfolio of creative work, it is a good idea to label these "Unpublished Concepts." This is true also for student exercises.

However, you will have to flesh out your ideas into fully formed, presentable, portfolio-worthy work. It is not enough to have a great idea. You must be able to show how your work could be executed effectively across a range of media.

See the exercise below for directions on how to create such a file of your best unpublished concepts.

Of course the best practice is to pretest creative concepts and executions. This testing can include A/B testing for headlines or e-mail message lines, or multivariate testing of several variables. If you can't get your idea presented, maybe you can get your idea tested.

The other, but often more difficult solution, is to leave the organization that is killing your soul. Find a different group that not only values new thinking, but actively encourages breakthrough ideas.

The Portfolio Exercise:

1. Create a physical binder and a digital folder for your unpublished concepts, designs, and writings.
2. Create a document or spreadsheet to catalog your concepts.
3. Add notes to your catalog describing, in detailed steps, the additional work that each concept requires to become portfolio ready.
4. For one of the concepts, estimate the hours needed to complete each step of the work required.
5. Using the Production Planning Time Line (see pp. 128–129), plan the days and times during which you will work on the further development and completion of your concept.

V. The JARGON Problem

Using design/creative language, not business language

"... CMYK with one PMS bump plate, plus inline spot matte..."

"...slab serif typeface with negative tracking and individually adjusted kerning..."

"...Tschichold's interpretation of Van de Graaf's canon.."

"...eliminating orphans, widows, and rivers..."

"...analogous rather than triadic color scheme..."

"...blind embossing..."

"...hi-res, HDR photos..."

"..WC3 and IAB compliant..."

"...improved ranking on SERP..."

I have often heard Creatives told that their work should speak for itself. This aphorism is only true when Creatives are speaking to other Creatives. However, when presenting their solutions to the Account Team, and especially when presenting to a client, the Creatives not only have to speak for their work, they have to do so in business language rather than in design jargon. The Creative Team has to explain how their creative work will accomplish business objectives. Without the correct language, all the Account Team, marketers, and clients may see and hear is a Creative making incomprehensible noises that will be viewed as little more than **POINTING AND GRUNTING** (see p. 154).

So rather than describe the aesthetics of color choices, a designer could speak about the benefit to the brand of "owning" a particular color in their market area, in order to increase recognition and recall.

Examples include Dodge "owning" red in the truck market, IBM being referred to as "Big Blue," and Prince "owning" the color purple.

A designer could also speak about the impact and memorability of a particular color, or the differentiation from other competitors. For example, if all the competitors in an industry use shades of blue and green, then using orange would be a visual differentiator.

Rather than refer to "voice," a copywriter could speak about authority, authenticity, or credibility.

Creatives need to explain how their work will work.

Avoiding jargon:

SAY THIS, NOT THAT

Every profession or specialized discipline has its own unique language. This jargon is not only a shorthand for communications between practitioners of that discipline, but is also a way in which people recognize and acknowledge that people belong in their group.

But when you are communicating with people outside your discipline, the jargon has to be translated into more conventional language to facilitate better comprehension by the listener and a more productive conversation.

Instead of this...	...say this:
• I like it	• It works -or- it doesn't work
• I'll play with this	• I'll work on this
• It's cool/hip/dope	• It is...
	- ...unique in the competitive space
	- ...consistent with the brand
	- ...relevant to the audience
	- ...memorable
	- ...impactful
	- ...testing well in recall

The Solution:

Build in a business rationale for your creative work, based on the Creative Brief. Make notes before your presentations, and review those notes to ensure that you are describing the effectiveness of your work in business terms rather than in creative terms.

The Two Presentations Exercise:

For a given piece of work, or design/creative assignment, develop two presentations. The first presentation is intended for other Creatives/writers/designers, and focuses on the aesthetics of the work. The second presentation is intended for a client, and focuses on the business purposes accomplished by the design.

VI. The POINT AND GRUNT Problem:

No creative rationale

I entered the conference room where I had been summoned by the Account Team. They were discussing final details of the budget before we submitted our proposal.

"We think we have some changes we'd like to see in the proposal design," explained Bill the account executive.

"Changes? You mean changes to the proposal document and contents including the campaign creative?" I asked, incredulously.

Bill nodded. "Yes."

I thought to myself, "You want to change the complex, handmade, custom proposal document that I am now in the midst of producing 12 copies of, and that I have shown you sketches, designs, and kept you informed of throughout the development process!!?"

However, what I said was, "I'll tell you what Bill. I'll give you my reasons for the document design looking and functioning the way it does. When I'm done, if you have better reasons for me to change to something else, I'll do so.

But if you don't have better reasons, then I'm leaving it the way it is. OK?"

"Um...sure. That's sounds OK," replied Bill.

I then proceeded to talk for about 15 minutes, giving the Creative Rationale for the size and shape of the proposal document; the choice of materials and colors; the weight and finish of the papers; the typeface choices and sizes; the interior layouts of individual pages, spreads, and gatefolds; the design and placement of the custom hand-cut tab dividers and pocket pages; and finally the contrast between our custom presentation and the work of our competition.

When I finished, I looked at Bill.

"That's perfect," said Bill.

"Thanks," I replied. "Let me know when you have the budget information completed so I can put that into the proposal."

I left the conference room.

Presenting a solid Creative Rationale that explains how the creative solution will deliver on the objectives of the Creative Brief (A2C) is essential. Copywriters choose the words they do because these specific words speak to the target audience. Art directors choose the mood, emotion, and conceptual constructs they do because these are the most effective way to achieve memorability, recall, audience engagement, and consumer interaction with the brand. Designers choose the typography, colors, and images they do to differentiate from the competition, speak to the brand, and achieve the specified objectives. And so on.

When Creatives do not describe the rationale for their decisions in business terms, they may only point and describe their work in words or jargon that, to the Account Team or client, are as meaningless as if they were merely grunting.

Presentation Skills

The ability to effectively present your ideas and your work is an essential skill for Creatives. There are some things to do, and things to avoid, both in what you say and what you do.

*See the complete list of **Essential Presentation Do's and Don'ts** on pages 178–179.*

The Solution:

As illustrated in the story on the preceding page, if you have clearly articulated the Creative Rationale as a part of the creative process, you will be able to explain how the creative work delivers on the objectives defined in the A2C Creative Brief.

If you develop your presentation skills so that you can persuasively and clearly present your work to an audience of decision makers, then your written Creative Rationale document and your presentation will be an effective combination.

The Creative Rationale Exercises:

1. Choose a project you have already created (written and/or designed). Take the Creative Brief or assignment directions, and write a rationale for explaining how each point in the brief delivers on the directions or objectives.

2. Present your project and Creative Rationale to a class or group. Take note of those instances where you are unable to provide a clear Creative Rationale. Revise your rationale accordingly. Remember this for next time.

3. Switch projects with another person, and develop a Creative Rationale for each other's work. Present the other person's work to a class or group.

VII. The ARTISTE Problem:

Using "I like it" rather than "it works

"I like it," said Ella the designer.

"Why do you like it?" I asked.

"Because it's cool," she replied.

"What makes it cool?" I asked.

"Um..." Ella paused.

"Exactly," I said.

I continued, "You have to be able to articulate to the client why this is great work. And it is really good. Your work is on brand, speaks to the target audience, and should deliver on the objectives defined in the brief. But you have to be able to explain that."

"Cool. I like that," she replied.

This problem is related to both The Point and Grunt Problem and The Romeo and Juliet Problem.

When you use "I like it" as a Creative Rationale, you are only describing your affective reaction to your work, not a thoughtful, cognitive response.

Asking the client, "Do you like it?" is another manifestation of **The ARTISTE Problem.**

A big part of selling to the brief is to present how the creative solution works to accomplish the objectives.

That is why Creatives should talk about how it "works" and never ask if someone "likes" it.

I call this **The ARTISTE Problem**, because creativity in this context is not about personal expression, but uniqueness AND effectiveness.

The other risk of asking a client if they "like it" is that they can always answer "no."

As I mentioned in the story at the beginning of this chapter (Introduction: The CREATIVES ARE JUST TOO "CREATIVE" Problems) people often have the mistaken notion that art is, and always has been, solely about personal expression. That is historically incorrect for the fine arts, and has never been the case for advertising and marketing Creatives.

The differences between
Art and Design, Writing and Copywriting

The difference between art and design is the subject of an ongoing and seemingly endless debate. I won't presume to explain that difference here.

But it is important to remember that even the ceiling of the Sistine Chapel was not solely a personal artisitic expression. Michelangelo (commercial artist) was commissioned (hired) for that project, and frequently disagreed with his patrons (clients).

The perceived diffferences between the practices of art and art direction/ design are often magnified; art is thought to be solely about personal expression, while art direction/design is solely about commerce. The perceived similarities are also magnified in part because visual designers are still referred to as the "art" department, and Art Director is a commonly used title. At one time "graphic design" was referred to as "commercial art." These terms confuse the issue of art versus design.

While it is generally understood that copywriting and other types of writing, novels and stories for example, are different, it is less commonly understood by those who are not writers that there are many types of copywriting, from print advertising, to TV commercials, to speeches, catalog copy, and many more. While these types of writing require certain similar skills, each of these requires a specific expertise to be successful.

In both writing and design, the techniques of storytelling and art are used. However the purposes for which these techniques are used can be different.

The Solution:

1. Never ask the client if they "like it."

2. Never say "I like it," unless you follow that up with
    "...because it works, and it works because it delivers
    on the objectives defined in the Creative Brief."

The "Correct Me" Exercise:
Agree with your colleagues and/or fellow students to correct each other when one of you says "I like it" or asks someone else if they "like it."

Then give them the opportunity to reword their question or statement.

This is how your effective use of language will eventually become a habit.

VIII. The LEAP OF FAITH Problem

No way to prove success

We were in a kickoff meeting for a new business pitch.

"What can we do to improve our odds of winning this account?" I asked Chuck, the account executive.

"Lower our price, Chuck replied.

"Other than that," I continued, "what can we do to demonstrate value to our client?"

"Lower our prices," said Chuck again.

Everyone in the room looked at me.

"Chuck," I began, "I have absolute confidence that you will be able to 'sharpen the pencil'

sharper than it has ever been before, and can quote a fee to the client that will seem like a bargain to them, but will still be profitable to us."

Chuck nodded.

"But what I need to know is, how can we prove to our client that what we will propose has been successful? Other than a low price, what would they actually find most valuable?"

"Oh..." said Chuck. "They want to increase their repeat business from their first-time customers."

"Great!" I said. "We can build in a way to measure that, to prove that our campaign has succeeded."

How will you prove that your solution has been successful? John Wanamaker, a pioneer in the department store business, is reputed to have said that half his advertising dollar was wasted; he just didn't know which half. Those days are long gone, and Creatives are expected to be able to build into their work the means to prove success, to

demonstrate **Return on Marketing Investment (ROMI)**. Otherwise you are asking the client to take a Leap of Faith that your solution will work.

Often Creatives focus on asking "how" something might be done. It is essential to also consider "why" something is to be done.

Return on Marketing Investment

Part of the ability to prove the financial effectiveness of a creative solution is being able to show the calculation of the Return on Marketing Investment. ROMI is a calculation of how much additional profit has resulted from a campaign, or specific advertising or marketing activity.

There are different ways of calculating ROMI. The differences depend on what costs are accounted for in the calculation, and what additional number of sales can be directly attributed to a specific advertising or marketing activity. The latter can be especially difficult to determine, as a consumer will be receiving multiple marketing messages simultaneously.

The basic formula is:

$$\frac{Gross\ Profit - Marketing\ Investment}{Marketing\ Investment} = ROMI$$

Of course, this requires a further understanding of the meaning of Gross Profit, how it is calculated, and how this differs from Net Profit. These subjects are outside the scope of this book.

The Solution:

The creative solution presented to a client should include a projected **Return on Marketing Investment**. It will be necessary to work closely with the Account Team to calculate the ROMI. The calculation of investment will include costs provided by the Creative Team. These can include labor hours, technical costs, and production costs. The profit margin and some other costs will be calculated by the Account Team.

See the sidebar on this page for how to calculate a projected **ROMI.**

The ROMI Exercise:

Using the formula above calculate the **ROMI** on a project.

Even though you will probably have to estimate some costs, you should research the costs of production and other elements to include in your ROMI calculation.

IX. The BAIT & SWITCH Problem

Changing direction without reselling the Account Team

"Are you ready for the presentation to the Account Team?" I asked Jeff the art director.

"Almost," he replied. "I'm just changing a few things."

"Changing what few things exactly?" I asked.

"Well I had this great idea last night, and it really is better. So I'm working on that."

"I'm glad you had a late night inspiration," I said. "Those can lead to some really great work."

"That's what I thought," said Jeff.

"But I have to ask, did you tell the Account Team about this change of direction?" I asked.

"Not yet," replied Jeff. "I was going to wait until I had it done."

"You should really talk to them now," I said.

"Really?" said Jeff.

"Tell me, Jeff, have you ever taken a bite of birthday cake expecting chocolate and been surprised by vanilla?"

Jeff nodded.

"That's what you're doing to the Account Team, and to the rest of the Creative Team," I said.

"I'll ask for a meeting ASAP," said Jeff.

"Good idea," I replied.

Once the Account Team has agreed to an approach, changing the direction of that approach without reselling this to the rest of the Creative Team and the Account Team will be a big problem.

This also presents a problem if the creative changes impact the budget for production or implementation.

This requirement applies to all involved. If the Account Team decides to change direction, they should first consult with the Creative Team.

There can be significant cost implications, since the Creative Team consists not only of a Copywriter and Art Director, but includes a media strategist and planner, a technologist, an interactive designer, an event planner, a videographer, and many more.

The Solution:
Always inform the rest of the Creative Team about any changes to the original plan or concept. Then, if the Creative Team and your Creative Director agree, inform the Account Team as well.

Factors that affect the
Costs of Production

As in the story on the first page of this chapter (p. 138), a seemingly minor change can introduce enormous complications into the production process. A change in color, paper, or even typeface can result in production delays and therefore increased costs.

Particularly since marketing communications is integrated across many forms of media, a change in one area will likely necessitate changes in many other areas.

Examples of factors likely to affect the costs of production:

Change of scope   *When the requirements of the project expand beyond the original understanding, costs will increase accordingly.*

Copy   *Copy changes are easier to make online in a content management based site, but can result in expensive reprinting of collateral material.*

Photography   *Photography may only be licensed for specific uses, incurring additional costs if used in areas not specified in the original agreement.*

Graphics   *If images are initially designed for the web in a lower resolution, then need to be recreated at a higher resolution for print, this will incur additional costs.*

The best practice is to keep the rest of your team informed of any potential changes, no matter what type of change you are making.

The Butterfly's Wings Exercise:*

On a collaborative project that involves a team of people, have one person pick something to change on their part of the project. Examine how that change would affect the work of the rest of the team, including design, copywriting, budgeting, media planning, and production. Then repeat this for each team member.

* The idea that a single butterfly could affect history was first described in Ray Bradbury's 1952 science fiction short story about time travel, "A Sound of Thunder."[1]

In 1960 meteorologist Edward Lorenz, in a presentation to the 139th meeting of the American Association for the Advancement of Science, proposed that the beat of a butterfly's wings on one side of the world could cause a storm on the other.[2]

The term "The Butterfly Effect" has come to refer to the idea that small changes in one place can have large effects elsewhere.

X. The PLAY IT SAFE Problem

Only presenting small ideas

"The client needs a new product information brochure for the sales force. Just like we did before," Jim the account manager began.

"How well did that work, Jim?" I asked. *"Were there improvements in the product knowledge among the sales force?"*

"There was improvement," Jim said assuredly.

"But yet their sales were flat. And in some regions they actually declined," I stated, pointing to the data.

"Yes, that's true. But we gave them good product training information," Jim said defensively.

"Perhaps the problem behind their declining sales is not the product training information, or the salesperson's understanding," I continued, *"It seems as though there is another cause at work here. Any ideas, Bob? Did the client say anything that might give us a clue as to their real problem?"*

"Um, not really."

"Tell you what Bob. Why don't we do some research, and then go back to the client with some relevant questions and possible solutions once we have identified some likely causes of their declining sales. In the meantime, we can, of course, produce whiz-bang product information materials for them."

Have **Big Ideas**. Big Ideas can be successfully executed with small budgets. But a small idea won't get bigger just by throwing money at it. If you find yourself in an agency where only small ideas are welcomed, and you stop presenting Big Ideas, or even having them, you are in a **SOUL KILLER** (p. 150) job, and you should look for opportunities elsewhere.

This is related to **The EINSTEIN Problem** (p. 168), in that a small idea is often simply repeating what has been done before.

Rather than thinking about a problem from the company's point of view, a good starting point is to imagine yourself as your client's customer. What does the customer think? How do they feel? What do they need?

The answer to the company's need is generally found by understanding what their customers need.

The differences between
UVPs and Big Ideas

A Unique Value Proposition (UVP) or Unique Sales Proposition (USP) is a statement of what a company or product offers in the marketplace that is different and distinctive, and of worth to consumers.

The UVP can be how a product functions, or how it looks, where it can be found, how much it costs, or a combination of these aspects. In this way, the UVP encompasses 3 of the 4 Ps of marketing, Price, Place, and Product.

A Big Idea is the unifying concept that drives the marketing efforts of a brand or product. A Big Idea is innovative and can transform the brand perception of the product. It is the example of how successful creativity in advertising is defined as something that is both original and useful. In this way the Big Idea belongs in the Promotion aspect of the traditional 4 Ps of marketing

Everyone now knows that Arm & Hammer® Baking Soda can be used to deodorize a refrigerator. But marketing this new use for their product beyond baking was a transformative Big Idea for that company, and led to many other new products and increased sales. This was a different solution than simply trying to sell more baking soda for its traditional use in baking.

The Solution:

Question everything. Especially question preconceived solutions, and unproven assertions about the nature of a problem. Ask for data. Require evidence. Ask questions.

The Digging for Info Exercise:

Pick a publicly traded company. Information, especially financial data, about such companies is more readily available than for privately held companies.

Research the company on www.hoovers.com, www.sec.gov, www.nasdaq.com, www.standardandpoors.com, or other sources of company information. Your librarian can direct you.

Look for the current and past performance of the company, its competitors, and projections for its future. Determine why the company is increasingly profitable, or gaining market share. If a company is losing market share or declining in profitability, do further research to determine the causes. Is it the economy? A change in the demographics of consumers? Something else?

XI. The ANTI-MUSKETEER Problem

Dis-integration of the execution

"The Advertising Team will present to the client first," said Dave, the advertising creative director.

"That's fine," replied Bill the account executive. "Just as long as the entire campaign works well across all media. Not like last time."

"What do you mean by that?" said Dave, accusingly.

"Well, last time, you changed the advertising at the last minute without telling the rest of the Creative Team. So that after the advertising presentation, all the other parts of the campaign looked like they belonged to a different strategy."

"Well, that won't happen this time," said Dave. "I'll let them all know what we are doing."

"You're just letting them know now?" said Bill with dismay.

"Well, they've got all night to catch up and be ready for tomorrow," said Dave, inconsiderately.

Sometimes in the course of creative development, the ideas of each part of the Creative Team — web, print, TV and radio advertising, events, social, and PR — will start to evolve. Eventually these separate executions can come to seem as if they are very different from each other. When this happens, all of the campaign creative is not working towards the same objectives. I call this **The ANTI-MUSKETEER Problem** (not all for one anymore).

Occasionally this problem occurs because of the self-absorption of one particular team's leader, as in the story above. More often, though, this happens because of the inherent problem solving that occurs within each discipline. Copywriters must craft language differently for print than for web, and imagery in print differs from that on a billboard or a web banner.

This problem solving can, however, result in a difference in the look and feel, and the messaging, of individual tactical executions in different media.

This is not an intentional, willful deviation from the agreed upon creative direction. Rather, this dis-integration is the expected result of different people working on the many different parts of a complex, multi-media campaign.

The principles of
Integrated Marketing Communications

One of the basic ideas of Integrated Marketing Communications (IMC) seems self-evident to most people when they first hear it: all the contacts a consumer has with a company or a brand should be consistent and relevant.

In practice, this means that every marketing or advertising communication from a company has a consistent message that is coordinated with all other messages.

That does not mean that all messages are identical, since the physical requirements of different media would make that impossible to achieve. For example, the words and images on a billboard that are viewed by a consumer for a few seconds as they drive by at 70 MPH cannot be the same as the those used in a catalog or product brochure that is meant to be read in detail.

Two other principles of IMC are less well known and obvious to the layperson. The first is that a company's structure must facilitate the integration of the marketing. If each product line has its own budget and marketing, the company's marketing will not be integrated.

The other principle is that each marketing communication tactic should be individually evaluated for effectiveness; each tactic directs a consumer to take some action, and these tactics combine in a chain to achieve the overall campaign objectives. Building this measurable, connected chain of tactics is another aspect of marketing communication integration.

The Solution:

In order to keep the campaign truly integrated, where all creative execution across different media are complementary, although not identical, it is necessary to have regular meetings to bring drifting executions back on track and working together.

The Disintegration Exercise:

On a team project to develop an integrated campaign, each media execution will be directed by a different person on the team.

Following the initial meeting to agree upon a creative direction, each team will only reassemble to present their individual contribution to the campaign.

Take note of how much or how little the different tactics support and coordinate with each other to create an integrated campaign.

XII. The WORST CHOICE Problem

1 2 X

Radding's Law: The likelihood that a client will pick the worst of three options is inversely proportional to the quality of the option

"I really like the third choice," said the client, much to our dismay.

Once we arrived back at our offices, Bill the account executive looked at me and said, "Don't say it."

"I don't really need to say it, do I?" I replied.

"No," said Bill. "But you could say 'I told you so' and be within your rights to do so."

"Well, I won't say it," I magnanimously replied, "as long as you promise never to put a bad

idea in front of a client again, assuming that they won't choose that option."

"You got it! Now how do we make this turkey fly?" Bill asked.

I sighed.

"Well...I have a couple of ideas, since I anticipated this outcome," I assured him.

Never, ever show a client a bad idea, assuming that they will never pick that idea. They almost always do. Whether the impetus to do so comes from the Creative Team or the Account Team, showing anything less than a workable solution is a bad practice.

Even if the client doesn't pick the bad idea, showing a bad idea undermines your credibility with the client. Clients assume, and rightly so, that you wouldn't show them anything that wasn't an effective solution.

I had a design professor who told us to always misspell a word in the first sentence. His reasoning was that a misspelled word would give the client something to fix, so that they would feel satisfied and leave the rest of the work alone.

This concept is known as **Hairy Arms**,[3] which is based on a story that Disney animators would add hair to the arms of character concepts so that their studio bosses would have something to critique, and would then leave the rest of their concepts unchanged.

My experience has shown exactly the opposite to be true. Once a client or anyone sees a mistake, their confidence in your attention to detail is diminished. Thereafter, the client will scrutinize every detail, and make unecessary changes where there are no mistakes.

Why I call it
Radding's Law
and Corollaries

When I first described the principle that, given a choice of options, the client was most likely to pick the worst one, my colleagues all nodded in agreement and chimed in with their own stories.

Even my friends in other professions told me that this principle was borne out by their own experience.

I was unable to find that this principle, although commonly understood, had a name. So I claimed it as Radding's Law.

My apologies to anyone who may have named this principle before I did.

But once I suggested this law, my colleagues and friends suggested several corollaries to Radding's Law:

*From architect Marilee Lloyd, AIA, **Lloyd's Corollary**: If the worst option is also the most expensive, the likelihood that the client will choose this option is reduced.*

*From chef Kay Jarrell, **Jarrell's Corollary**: The most minor problems produce the greatest number of negative customer comments.*

The Solution:
We come back to having a Creative Rationale for your choices, concepts, and executions.

When presenting multiple solutions, each one should have its own distinct Creative Rationale.

The Three Different Rationales Exercise:
Develop three completely different solutions for a problem or project assignment. Each solution should have a distinct Creative Rationale. Present these three solutions. Repeat until this becomes your regular method of working, not merely an exercise.

XIII. The EINSTEIN Problem

Vetoing an idea because it is too hard to sell

"I can't present that to the client," protested Sam the account executive. "He simply won't understand it. "

"I'm sure I can explain it to him," I offered.

"But it's not like anything they've ever done before," Sam continued. "It will scare him."

"I understand that," I said, reassuringly. But our client is also scared of not getting the results he needs."

"How does that help us?" asked Sam.

"We can convince our client that he is more scared of failing than he is of trying a new approach," I explained.

"We can convince him," I continued, "that simply doing the same thing he has been doing is likely to continue to fail."

"That might work," said Sam.

"It might. But doing the same thing and expecting a different result is the definition of...well, you know the rest," I said.

"The rest of what?" asked Sam.

The Account Team might veto an idea because they don't understand how to sell it to the client. Depending on the agency and the team, this is more likely to occur with a particularly new, or big, idea. I call this **The EINSTEIN Problem,** because Albert Einstein is reported to have said, "Insanity is doing the same thing over and over again and expecting different results."*

Sometimes the clients ask for an "out of the box" solution; the first thing to understand is how they define "the box."

A client's definition of the "box" is often much more limited or conventional than that of the Creative Team.

Therefore, what is outside the client's definition of a "box" is still inside the what the Creatives perceive as a "box."

A client may think that the "box" is the specific color they have been using for many years, and changing that color is a radical and highly creative suggestion. This example actually happened to me.

Creatives are generally starting with a larger definition of what is possible. So when they get the charge to think outside the box, Creatives will really push those limits. A new idea that challenges people's preconceptions can be difficult to accept.

* This quotation is generally attributed to Einstein, but has also been attributed to Benjamin Franklin, Mark Twain, and Rita Mae Brown. Since there is no definitive attribution, and Einstein is the most widely credited for this statement, I named the problem for him.

Big New Concept

Broadly speaking, there are two categories of marketing: short-term marketing and sales; and longer-term marketing, growth, and brand building.

Both kinds of marketing are important. If a company does not bring in enough revenue to sustain their business, they won't survive long enough to build their brand. However, a company can also damage their brand by pursuing short-term profitability in a way that is contrary to the company's principles, reputation, and intended brand image.

This key to selling a new Big Idea that a client may find challenging, and even a little scary, is to frame the solution as addressing BOTH the short-term profitability and the long-term brand building.

Of course, the Creative Rationale has to explain how the solution effectively achieves this dual purpose. And, of course, the Creative Rationale has to address the issues presented in the A2C Creative Brief.

Therefore, a better A2C Creative Brief results in a better C2A Creative Rationale, which provides the justification to the client for buying a big new concept.

The Solution:
Write a Creative Rationale that clearly explains the business benefits of a particular creative solution.

The Competitive Rationale Exercise:
Develop a Creative Rationale for an existing product. Explain in business terms why the product has certain attributes, such as size, shape, and color. Explain the business value of the graphics and typography on the product and its packaging.

Now do the same for a direct competitor of the first product.

Which product has a competitive advantage? Why?

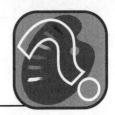

XIV. The I MAY NOT KNOW ART, BUT... Problem

Vetoing an idea you think they won't like

"He won't like it," insisted Sue the account executive.

"We've discussed this before," I began. *"It's not about whether he likes it or not, but whether it will work."*

"Yes, I know that," replied Sue. *"But the client doesn't know that."*

"What the client does know is that improved results will make him look like a hero to his boss," I countered.

"Yes, he's scared of his boss," agreed Sue.

"And we can use that to convince our client that liking is irrelevant," I continued. *"Results that will impress his boss are what's most important!"*

"Then let's agree to never ask our client if he 'likes' something, because one rule of salesmanship is..."

"...never ask a client a question to which he can answer 'No'," Sue completed.

Those who are untrained in Creative will often state their reactions to creative work as "liking" or "not liking" the work.

Creatives are trained (or should be trained) through participation in seemingly endless critiques to express positive or negative opinions about creative work as "it works" or "it doesn't work" and be able to provide reasons why.

The venerable Latin saying *de gustibus non est disputandum* is still true: there is no point debating about matters of taste.

In matters of taste about, for example, flavors of ice cream, there is no dispute. Saying "I like it" or "I don't like it" is relevant. In such things, people are the experts on their own preferences and tastes.

But in the context of advertising and marketing communications, taste is not the exclusive determinant of effectiveness. And while "liking" is an indicator of positive affect towards a particular creative execution, the tastes of the account executive or the client may not be the same as those of the target audience for the creative work.

The differences between
I Think and I Feel

"I think I like it."   *"I feel that this is a better idea."*

*These are examples of what **not** to say. Or rather, how **not** to say it.*

Replacing "I like it" from your vocabulary with "It works because..." is a useful habit for creative professionals to develop when speaking or writing about their work. This word usage is also an important habit for the Account Team to develop.

A related issue is the misuse of "I think" when describing how you feel, and saying "I feel" when describing your thinking. One reason for avoiding "I like it" is that it is an emotional response, rather than a cognitive one.

Use "think" when you are talking about ideas, and "feel" when you are talking about emotions.

However, eliminate "I think" when you are stating your conclusions. You are more persuasive when you simply state your conclusions without this qualifier.

The Solution:

Focus your efforts on an accurate determination of the client's real problems, and then on gaining insights into the sources of these problems. Do this whether or not your agency can provide the solution. In this way you will become a valued counselor to the client, not simply a provider of a creative product.

Include these insights in the A2C brief, and sell the client on the solution to their problems that will work, even if the client doesn't "like" it.

The Survey Exercise:

Develop a simple survey. This can be either in print form or using one of several free online survey tools.

Pick a product. Ask questions about how the product is used, and why that product was chosen by consumers rather than any of the competitive products. Were the decisions based on price? Perhaps on the brand name? Consider these insights when developing your own creative rationales for your work.

XV. The IF MAN WAS MEANT TO FLY Problem

Vetoing an idea they don't understand

"No," said Tim the account executive firmly. "I can't present this to the client."

"Why not?" I asked.

"He won't understand what you are trying to do with this, or how it will work," Tim answered.

"Tell me Tim," I asked. "Do you understand how this will work?"

"The client has never tried anything like this before," Tim non-answered.

"But do you understand?" I asked again.

"The client is expecting something like what we did for them before, so that's what we have to give them," Tim continued.

"As I showed you," I replied, "we have that option to present. But this other solution will work better, which will make him happy. And when the client is happy, I know that you are happy."

"No, the client won't like it," Tim said with a degree of finality.

"That's certainly true if you don't understand this well enough to present." I continued, more than a bit irritated, but trying not to show it.

The conventional option was the only one presented to the client. We did not get the project, which was awarded to another agency that presented a unique solution.

Although the Account Team may say that the client doesn't "like" the idea, perhaps the Account Team simply doesn't understand how the idea will work to solve their client's problems.

In that case, it may be that the Creatives haven't explained the solution as well as they need to, in terms of how they are solving the client's business problem (see The JARGON Problem, p. 152).

The Creative Team has to sell their solution to the Account Team, before the Account Team can sell the solution to their client.

When the Creative Team enables the Account Team's success, and vice versa, everyone benefits.

When the Account Team presents the same solutions that their client has seen before, or has come to expect, that sameness reduces the value of an agency's services to that of a commodity that is bought for the lowest price, rather than elevating the agency's brand quality to one that can command a premium price.

Specifications & Expectations

The directions tell you which way to go, but not how far to go.

So you should always meet the specifications of a project, but exceed the expectations.

Specifications can include physical dimensions, file size and download time, or other fixed attributes.

However, even some specifications can be based on an assumption of what the solution will be, because of what has been done before. So consider if the specifications are essential. But remember to keep the rest of your team informed if your solution deviates from the specs.

So remember to follow the project directions, but go further than expected.

The Solution:

The Creative Team should provide a Creative Rationale that clearly explains the value of their proposed solution in business terms, so that the Account Team can use this rationale to sell the work to their client.

The Selling to the Brief Exercise:

To provide an opportunity to practice "selling to the brief," students should present a project to a jury of instructors and students. The presentation should include how the solution meets specifications while exceeding the expectations set forth in the project directions (i.e., the brief for that project).

The presentation should be followed by questions from the jury. This will be challenging for the presenter, but is a proven method for improving the understanding of what information is needed for a persuasive, winning presentation. Regular presentations also improve the recoginition that preparation is essential for success.

The C2A Briefing Solutions

Two Account Team and Eight Creative Team Steps to
Enable Account Success

In this chapter I have described the many problems that can occur during the
C2A briefing and the steps that follow.

I have summarized solutions to these problems. However, as in the A2C
Briefing Problems, these solutions must become a regular practice so as to
prevent the occurrence of the problems.

Changing an existing way of working first requires analysis, understanding,
and commitment. This must be followed by diligent practice, so that a new
process becomes a habit.

Account Team:
TWO STEPS TO SUCCESS During the C2A Briefing

A summary of the solutions to Account Team C2A problems

The Account Team can facilitate their own success by using these steps that enable the Creative Team to develop their best solutions.

1. **Give the Creatives a real voice:**
   Listen to their ideas. Encourage their unconventional, uncomfortable, challenging ideas. Then require that they help the Account Team craft a method to succesfully sell the solution to the client.

2. **Make the Creatives prove it:**
   Require that the Creative Team provide a Creative Rationale for their proposed solutions. Facilitate their ability to develop such a rationale by providing the necessary information and insights during the A2C Briefing.

Creative Team:
EIGHT STEPS TO SUCCESS During the C2A Briefing

A summary of the solutions to Creative Team C2A problems

1. **Words+Images+Media should be complementary, not redundant**

   This is a basic principle of effective advertising. This is in contrast to the old presentation principle of "show them what you're telling, and tell them what you're showing." The images should complement and complete the meaning of the copy, just as the copy should explain the meaning of the images.

2. **Focus on the target audience(s)**

   Practice empathy. Imagine yourself as a member of the target audience. What do you think and feel? Validate this imagining with research and testing. Change your concepts as needed to work for the audience.

3. **Don't insult your audience**

   Respect the intelligence and comprehension of your audience. While the words of H. L. Mencken* may still be pertinent for some businesses or politics, you will do better by expecting more from your audience.

4. **Meet the timeline and budget**

   Joe's First Rule** is "Never, ever miss a deadline." But you need to make sure that the deadline is correct and accurate (see The I'M NOT YOUR SLACKER FRIEND Problem, p. 112). But don't have the final deadline as your only target date. Develop a production timeline (see The Production Planning Timeline, pp. 128–129). If you have a budget, specified in either hours or a dollar amount, estimate your expenditure of time and/or money before you begin work. If there is likely to be a problem, notify your supervisor as soon as possible. Don't wait to raise the alert until you have spent 90% of your budgeted time or money, and find that you still have 50% of the work left to do.

---

* *H. L. Mencken (American journalist, editor, and social critic, 1880–1956) wrote, "No one in this world...has ever lost money by underestimating the intelligence of the great masses of the plain people. Nor has anyone ever lost public office thereby."* [4]

** *Joe's Rules are a collection of rules and principles I give to students and colleagues (see pp. 202-204). These rules summarize my experiences and lessons I learned being a creative professional.*

5. Provide alternative solutions

Have more than one workable idea. Have a solid Creative Rationale for each solution that you present to your client. Never present a solution that will not be effective (see The Worst Choice Problem, p. 168). A useful tool for developing alternative ideas is Osborne's Checklist (see p. 82).

6. Have a solution that works across all media

Have solutions that can be applied in any medium. Consider how a solution will work in different media when you are developing your ideas.

7. Have a solution that has "legs"

Develop ideas that can last beyond the immediate problem you are addressing. Develop solutions that can have longevity beyond the immediate need.

8. Deliver a Creative Rationale in business language

Clearly explain how your creative work solves business problems for your client, rather than using jargon, by demonstrating:

a) Competitive differentiation

Explain how your creative work helps the client's brand to stand out among the competition, and presents a unique and distinctive value to the client's customers.

b) Brand perception (i.e., on brand)

Explain how your creative work is true to the brand perception that consumers have of your client's company, or advances your client's brand closer to where it is intended to be. This type of work is referred to as being "on brand."

c) Originality

Explain how your creative work is unique rather than a rework or imitation of another company's marketing or previous work you created.

d) The ability to measure effectiveness, and thereby to prove ROMI, is designed into the work

Explain how the effectiveness of your creative work can be measured. Explain how your creative work contributes to the overall success of the campaign or the company's goals.

Essential PRESENTATION DO'S and DON'TS*

The ability to effectively present your ideas and your work is an essential skill for Creatives. There are things to do, and things to avoid, both in what you say and what you do.

Do Tell a Story

A story is more memorable and engaging than a lecture. Framing your presentation in the form of a story can be an effective method. This is one reason that marketers create customer avatars (detailed profiles of a company's ideal target customers) and build stories around these profiles.

Do Enunciate

Pronouncing words clearly is a skill that can be developed. When presenting in a large room to a large group of people, it can be necessary to overarticulate the endings of words in a way that will sound exaggerated to the people standing next to you, but will make your speech more comprehensible to the people in the audience.

Do Use Business Language

See Step 8 of "Creative Team, Eight Steps to Success During the C2A Briefing" on pp. 177.

Do Move with Intention

An effective presentation technique can be to speak while standing in one spot, then to move a few steps while speaking. Then stop, stand in another spot, and continue to speak.

This is also an effective way of handing off the presentation to a teammate. Once you arrive in the new spot, you conclude speaking, and your teammate begins their part of the presentation.

Do Rehearse

Practice will enable you to present with more confidence. The solutions presented in a confident presentation are more likely to be perceived by the audience as effective. Rehearsals reduce the temptation to read from the screen, or overrely on reading from notes.

Rehearsals are especially important for a team presentation so that each person's part can be well coordinated and timed to work well with others. Many client presentations will have a set time limit, and rehearsal is necessary to be able to meet that limitation.

Do...

...keep your chin up so people can see your face and hear your voice. Speaking with your chin down, as when you are reading from your notes, will direct the sound of your voice into the floor, and make it harder for your audience to hear you clearly.

...have energy, because an energetic delivery implies that you are excited about your work. Adjust your volume to the size of the room, so that you are neither to loud for the room or your team, or too quiet to be heard.

* Style guides and grammar usage reference books don't agree on one correct way to write "do and don't" as plurals. While an apostrophe is generally not used to indicate a plural, in some cases the use of an apostrophe will enhance readability, and is considered an acceptable form.

Don't Meander

Don't nervously shift your weight from foot to foot. This makes your audience nervous and undermines their confidence in your ideas.

Don't thigh slap

It is common to gesture while speaking. When you are done speaking to a group of people, don't simply let your hands drop to your sides and make a slapping sound against your thighs. This noise upstages the person who is speaking, and distracts your audience from what is being said. Just as theater actors are trained to continue being "in character" even when they are not speaking, it is important to recognize that you are still "on stage" even when your part of the presentation is complete.

No "tchutching"

When some people speak, they allow their tongue to smack against the roof of their mouths when ending a sentence or while preparing to take a breath. This "tchutching" noise is distracting and unprofessional.

Don't...

...point at the client.

This is generally considered aggressive and rude, and is the reason that most politicians gesture with a thumb up, loosely clenched hand instead.

...read from the screen.

This action turns your face away from the audience and makes you harder to hear. You also look unprepared.

...be too loud.

Adjust the level of your voice to the size of the room and the volume of the other people with whom you are presenting.

...be too quiet.

Again, adjust your volume appropriately.

...say that you "like" it, or ask if they "like" it.

See The ARTISTE Problem on p. 156.

The C2A Briefing Solutions Exercises

Exercise 1: The Process Book

A **Process Book** is a binder into which everything related to a course is placed. This includes the syllabus, class notes, research, concepts, rough drafts, digital backup and archive copies, and finished work.

The purpose of creating a process book is to develop the habit of keeping complete records of client project work, whether as a Creative or member of an Account Team.

For every client project, I create a binder where I keep all my notes, hard copies of all e-mails, sketches, research, and other relevant information. I organize this binder with clearly labeled tabs, and a label on both the front of the binder and the spine including the project number and client name so the binder can be easily distinguished from others while sitting on a shelf. The tabs mirror the computer file folders I also create at the start of the job. When the job is complete, I burn all my files to a disc or drive, and place this storage medium in the binder for archiving.

Invariably, students ask questions that are already answered in the syllabus. I ask them, "If you had been in a client meeting where these questions were answered, would you call the client every time you wanted an answer? Or would you look in your notes from the meeting where the question was already answered?" I then direct them to the syllabus, which is an element that should be in their process book.

Creating and using a process book helps builds the habit of creating a professional record-keeping process.

Instructions:

1. Create a three-ring binder process book for each course.

2. Place a label on the front of the binder, and another on the spine of the binder, with Your Name, Course Number and Title, and Semester.

3. Create section tabs with these clearly readable labels:

   - **Syllabus:** a hard copy of the syllabus
   - **Lecture notes:** your notes from class arranged chronologically
   - **Handouts:** any supplemental material your instructor handed out in class
   - **E-mails:** hard copies arranged chronologically
   - **Research:** web, library, references list
   - **Concepts:** in written form
   - **Thumbnails:** initial concepts with description of thought process
   - **Progression**: digital design progression and/or written drafts by date
   - **Final**: final versions of designs and/or final version of paper(s)

4. Add additional tabs as needed for your own purposes. Your instructor may choose to require additional tabs, and may evaluate your process books at the midterm and at the end of the course.

Exercise 2: How to Participate in a Critique

The best resource I have found about participating in a critique is on the website of the AIGA, the professional association for design.[5]

A simplified summary of the rules are listed below. Following that are instructions for how to master these rules.

What a critique is not
A critique is not an occasion to show off your skill at insulting other people. Neither is it an opportunity to BS the instructor and the other students. It is not an opportunity to engage in ad hominem attacks, nor to be condescending.

What a critique is
A critique is an opportunity to both give and receive what is usually referred to as constructive criticism. It is an opportunity to be both honest and helpful, by focusing on the effectiveness of the work.

The Rules, Simplified:
As the presenter
- Be prepared
- Have your work ready to present
- Have a creative rationale ready to present (see p. 147)
- Focus on the work
- Be open to improvement
- Don't be defensive
- Take notes

As a Critic
- Contribute to a postive group effort
- Start with what works, then move on to what could be improved
- Separate concept from execution
- Point out several conceptual ideas that could be improved upon without giving specific instructions for execution

Instructions:
1. For a specific creative project, each person or group presents their work.

2. The presenters have a set amount of time to describe:
   - The assignment or problem
   - Their concept or strategy
   - The specifics of the execution of the concept
   - The Creative Rationale that validates the execution of the concept

3. Then the other students ask questions for a set amount of time. The presenter is given time to respond to each question. To maximize the value of this part of the critique, this Q&A should be approached as a discussion between the questioners and the presenter.

4. The presenter should take notes on the comments, either during the critique or immediately following.

5. The instructor should moderate the critique session for effectiveness, civility, honesty, and time management.

Chapter Notes

1. Bradbury, Ray. (1952). *A Sound of Thunder.* Springfield, OH: Crowell-Collier Publishing Co.

2. Lorenz, Edward. (1972). Transcript of speech presented at the American Association for the Advancement of Science. Retrieved from http://eaps4.mit.edu/research/Lorenz/Butterfly_1972.pdf

3. Frease, Jessica. (2014). Transcript from "All Things Considered." Retrieved from http://www.npr.org/2014/11/17/364760847/whats-with-all-of-the-hairy-arms-in-graphic-design (original work broadcast November 17, 2014).

4. Mencken, H. L. (1926). "Notes on Journalism." *The Chicago Tribune.* Retrieved from http://archives.chicagotribune.com/1926/09/19/page/87/article/notes-on-journalism

5. Cheng, Karen. (20121) *How to Survive a Critique: A Guide to Giving and Receiving Feedback.* Retrieved from http://www.aiga.org/how-to-survive-a-critique/

Chapter 9

Now What? Next Steps

How to get there from where you are now

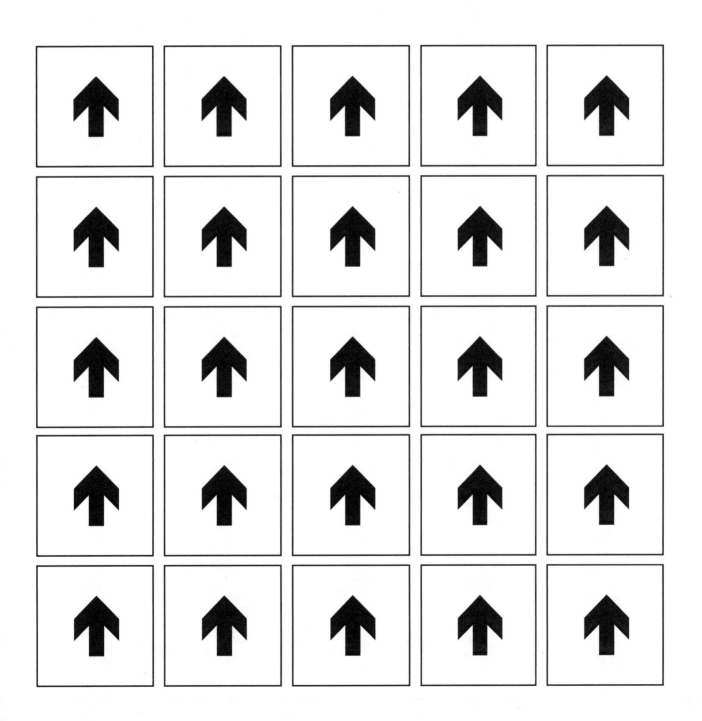

Introduction: Now What? Next Steps

How to get there from where you are now

"We have an opportunity with a new client," said Rob the account executive. *"Have you got time to talk about it?"*

"Absolutely," I replied enthusiastically. *"I just got your email a little while ago. It looks like it has great possibilities."*

"I think we should include Deb from research and Phil from events," said Rob. *"Let me send you the preliminary brief for your input."*

"Thanks," I replied.

"Who else do you think we should bring in on this?" asked Rob.

"Well," I began. *"I'll be there for Creative. Without blowing the budget early, I think that Jill the technologist should be in on this. And Sue from Social. Between us we should be able to assess further needs.*

"Perfect," replied Rob. *"I'll have Amy go into the online scheduler and set up a time when everyone is available."*

"Sooner is better than later," I added. *"If we have to schedule something early or late to make it happen, that's OK."*

"Thanks," said Rob. *"I'll also send out the preliminary brief to everyone before we meet. I also have some other relevant background and competitive info to include."*

"Excellent," I said. *"I'm really looking forward to this one."*

"Me too," said Rob. *"See you at the meeting."*

As this story illustrates, the perennial, clichéd conflict between "Suits" and "Creatives" does not have to be the norm.

The stories and problems I describe in this book may leave the impression that a cooperative, collaborative, positive agency work experience is an unattainable fantasy.

However, the very best agencies today, doing the most innovative and successful work for their clients, are also among the best run, most collaborative companies.

Consider this book to be a way of helping you recognize situations that can be improved. The steps in this chapter, in addition to the problem-specific solutions in Chapters 7 and 8, describe some of the ways you can work with your colleagues to build a more effective working relationship. In doing so, you will contribute to building a more successful agency.

Introduction: Now What? Next Steps

How to get there from where you are now

NEXT STEPS

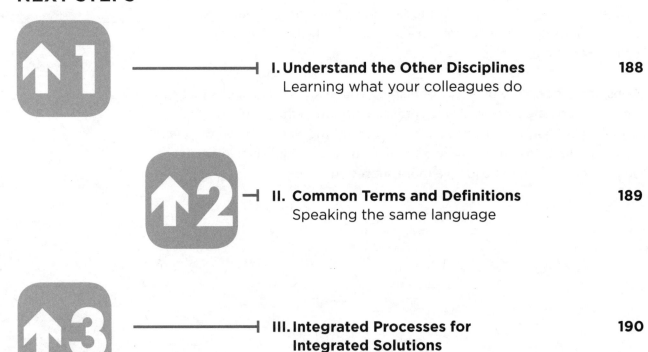

RESOURCES

I. Understand Other Disciplines

Learning what your colleagues do

As mentioned earlier, every agency has their own version of processes and responsibilities. The relationship between the disciplines will be affected by the organizational structure of the company, and by the styles and personalities of the people employed there.

As in any organization, this can result in constant misunderstandings, and people being at odds with each other.

To introduce people to all the functions of the agency so as to increase their understanding and appreciation of all the agency's functions, new agency employees often started in the traffic department, where they made certain the work moved from department to department, getting the necessary input and approvals.

The Steps:

1. When you join an agency, learn the processes of the entire agency. Learn the process of different disciplines. Learn what other people do, how they do it, and what they think and feel about it.

2. Walk around the agency and take notes on where people are located, and what they do. Find out who you can ask questions. Get an organizational chart, and identify the people you have spoken to.

3. If the agency's processes are documented, take notes on the differences between how the documentation describes the process and what people actually do. There is always a difference.

4. If the processes are not documented, then start your own documentation. Keep notes on the steps you and other people take to accomplish the work. Write your own process documents, then modify them as necessary when you see ways to improve the process.

5. Increase your understanding of the entire agency, and how your work contributes to everyone else's success, and the success of the agency. This will help your own work to be more collaborative, relevant, and effective, and your work experience to be more enjoyable.

II. Common Terms and Definitions

Speaking the same language

Having gained an understanding of the other disciplines and the entire agency, use that knowledge to speak in a common language of purpose, with a focus on the work.

The Steps:

1. Be aware of your own jargon, and the jargon of other disciplines in the agency. If you are unfamiliar with a term, write it down. Then ask what the term means, or look it up. Don't assume that you know the meaning of an unfamiliar term. Even a common word can have a very different meaning in a new context.

2. Learn the jargon of your clients. All clients have their own unique terms and definitions. Ask the copy editors if you have a question, since they are the ones who will have a mastery of the language of the agency's clients.

3. Develop common terminology when none exists.

4. Avoid clichés. While linguistic shortcuts can be useful, the overuse of clichés can lead to misunderstanding.

III. Integrated Processes for Integrated Solutions ⬆3

Bringing the teams together

Don't impose your ideas for a better process on people in a different discipline. Understand how they work and what improvements they would make. Then share with them how you work and what you would change.

Then work together to develop a process that everyone agrees to try. And keep making improvements as circumstances and needs change.

Focus on results and agree on the timeline, the intermediate checkpoints, and the deadlines, but don't manage the methods by which people accomplish their tasks.

The Steps:
1. Enlist people from other disciplines to willingly participate.

2. Ask questions.

3. Collect information.

4. Compare the processes of different disciplines.

5. Find the interfaces between the disciplines.

6. Draft a comprehensive process.

7. Ask for comments.

8. Make changes.

9. Ask for more comments.

10. Make final changes.

11. Try the process.

12. Review the results.

13. Make changes.

14. Keep going.

IV. What They Ask For PLUS What They Need

Solving underlying problems

Four particular problems are worth restating as principles for a long-term approach to your work. These are **The WRONG PRESCRIPTION Problem**, p. 102; **The WRONG DIAGNOSIS Problem**, p. 104; **The EVERY TOOL IS A HAMMER Problem**, p. 106; and **The TAKING THE WRONG PRESCRIPTION Problem**, p. 148.

Ask questions to dig deeper into the causes of a client's situation. Don't simply treat the symptoms of perceived problem. Seek to understand and address the causes.

The Steps:

1. Question assumptions.

2. Research information about clients, consumers, observers, competitors, the domestic and world economy, and the impact of regulation and trade.

3. Look for insights into client and audience behavior, motivation, and decision making.

4. Think about the implications and consequences of your research findings.

5. Present your findings and larger implications.

6. Work with your colleagues to develop solutions to the underlying causes as a means of addressing the symptoms.

V. Prove It

Demonstrating value

As mentioned in **The LEAP OF FAITH Problem**, p. 158, it is not enough to guess, or presume, that you know how well your proposed solution will perform. It is not enough to guess how well it did perform after it was produced.

You have to prove it.

Pretesting helps ensure the likelihood of success. Post-testing provides proof of success.

The proof has to be defined in terms of how the objectives were originally stated. Therefore the original objectives have to be numerically specific and have a clear time frame.

The Steps:

1. Make certain that the objectives of a campaign are clear, numerically specific, and with a clearly defined time frame.

2. Make certain that each tactic that will be used in combination to achieve the overall campaign objectives is pretested.

3. Make certain that each tactic has a measurement mechanism built in from the beginning.

4. Monitor the progress of each tactic for performance during the campaign.

5. Revise or eliminate underperforming tactics.

6. Evaluate the success of each tactic at the end of the campaign.

7. Evaluate the success of the overall campaign.

8. Present your proof of success to the client and use it as an example of the quality of your work.

The Next Steps Exercises

Unlike the earlier exercises in this book, think of these next steps as more long-term projects. These exercises will not be completed in an hour or so; nor will you finish them in a day or a week.

Rather, these are meant to be ongoing efforts at learning and improvement.

Come back to these exercises as you progress in school, in your career, and in your profession. Use these ideas to inform your own professional development. Then make up your own Next Steps, and keep going.

Exercise 1: More Role Switching

Earlier in this book (see p. 56) there is an exercise about switching roles with people in other disciplines.

This long-term exercise is about finding other ways to learn about different disciplines, jobs, and aspects of the marketing and advertising professions.

1. If you are studying the business of advertising, volunteer to help the people developing the creative communication in a student group or other organization, such as a charity.

2. If you are studying design or writing, volunteer to help the treasurer of a student group. Volunteer to help the advertising sales manager of your college publication. Volunteer to work on the promotion of theater productions or concerts.

In short, learn everything you can about not only your own chosen profession, but as much as you can about the associated professions with which you will be collaborating during your career.

The Next Steps Exercises

Exercise 2: Start your own agency

Networking is an often overused word in advertising, and in business in general. However, associating with people who are good at what they do, whatever that may be, is always beneficial.

When you find skilled people with whom you could work, it is important to take note of the possibilities.

Great agencies are often started by colleagues from different disciplines who share a common vision of the type of work they want to do. They share a compatible approach to work. They are driven to do better each day. They appreciate people with expertise in other areas.

1. Keep in touch with the people you meet along the way. Stay connected to your classmates from school. Ask people what they are doing, and congratulate them on their successes, promotions, and new jobs.

2. Pay attention to the skills of people in other disciplines than yours. The skills to start a successful agency, and keep it going, take time to acquire. Not everyone has the temperament to run a small business.

3. Be open to the possibility of a new situation, and seize the opportunity. It may lead you to starting your own consulting practice or agency.

4. Find good people in other disciplines with whom you can work effectively, and who have the interest, drive, and temperament to work in a start-up agency.

5. Where will you get the start-up funding you need? Will you have a relationship with a company who will agree to become your first client? Will that agreement be sufficient for a bank to lend you start-up money? Will you, as many small businesses do, get your family to invest?

6. Decide how your agency will be structured. Will it be a single-owner business, a partnership, or some type of corporation?

7. Find clients you can help. Create great work. Pay your bills. Build your agency's brand.

Exercise 3: Networking

Despite the clichés in movies, effective networking is not accomplished by a massive exchange of business cards at a cocktail party. Real networking is not an event, but is a process.

Build your network over time from the people you work with. Include classmates with whom you successfully collaborate on projects. Include mentors and teachers. Include colleagues and supervisors whom you would like to work with again.

Remember that building a network of people you trust, and who also trust you, takes time.

The Steps:
1. Keep a file, spreadsheet, list, or notebook containing the contact information of people with whom you study or work.

2. Keep in touch on social media, email, or by letter (some people still do write letters!). Or send them a postcard when you travel, and a greeting card on holidays and birthdays.

3. When an opportunity arises to recommend someone you know who is qualified for a job or a freelance assignment, do so.

4. Write letters of recommendation when you can honestly do so.

5. Ask for advice from people in your network who are more experienced than you are in a specific area.

6. Send thank you cards, letters, and emails.

7. Keep building your trusted network.

Chapter 10

Conclusion

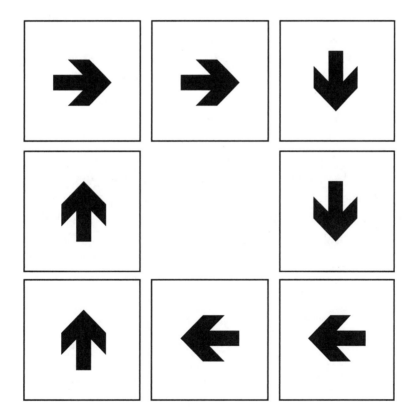

Conclusion

This book is about effectively collaborating to produce better work.

One benefit of effective collaboration, both with your colleagues and with clients, is that your workplace experience will be a more congenial and satisfying one.

This is beneficial not only to you, but to clients who will get more effective results, and to an agency's management who will have more satisfied and loyal employees. Satisfied employees tend to stay with a company, while unhappy employees tend to leave, taking their abilities and client relationships with them to competitors.

Anyone who has years of work experience has been in at least one negative, non-collaborative work environment. While this book cannot prevent those negative experiences from happening, I hope that the content will help you recognize those situations sooner. In that way perhaps you can avoid them, have the tools with which to improve the situation, or remove yourself expeditiously to a more positive workplace.

If you have experiences related to the content of this book I hope you will contact me. If you encounter other problems that I did not describe, or have other examples or stories illustrating the problems and solutions, please also write to me at josephradding@gmail.com.

If you find the problem identifications useful, or find the solutions applicable, and especially if you develop your own solutions to these problems, I would like to hear from you.

I hope that together, we can all make great work, and enjoy the process.

Joe's Rules

Joe's Rules

39 Rules for Work and Life

These are personal rules I developed for my own use over many years and have also shared with students.

Remember that the point of any list of rules is as a starting point for developing your own.

1. Never, ever, ever miss a deadline.

2. Make certain that the deadline is real.

3. Have reasons, not excuses.

4. When you are thinking about your work, you must have a pencil in hand and paper ready, otherwise you are only "thinking about thinking."

5. Start your work with a pencil, not a computer.

6. Get up from the computer once each hour to stretch and look out the window to the horizon. Do this for 2 minutes, and then get back to work.

7. Stand and sit with your ears aligned with your shoulders, otherwise working at a desk or computer will hurt after a short time.

8. Do more work.
    The antidote to Sturgeon's Law ("95% of everything is crap") is to do more work. That way you will have more of the good 5% to show for your efforts.

9. Be on time (see Rule #1)
    Remember that early is on time, on time is late, and late is unacceptable.

10. Teach.
    To truly master a subject, you must teach it to others.

11. The directions tell you which way to go, but not how far to go. That is up to you.

12. Meet the specifications, exceed the expectations.

13. Focus on the process (see Rule #18) and a good product is more likely to result. Ignore the process, and the product will be disappointing.

14. Learn to speak for your work and give reasons for every decision you make. Your work will only "speak for itself" when you are showing it to others in your profession. When you are presenting to people outside your profession, you must speak for your work. (see Rule #3)

15. Learn as much about your client's business as you can, before you meet them.

16. Learn as much about a potential employer as you can, before you meet them.

17. Do the best work of which you are capable.

18. Remember the Creative Process (see Rule #12):

    a. Define the problem
    b. Research
    c. Develop solutions/ideation
    d. Test solutions
    e. Refine solutions
    f. Produce/implement solutions
    g. Measure the results
    h. Refine the solution further

19. Always have your business cards and your elevator pitch ready.

20. Always carry an "idea book," or sketch book. The faintest ink is better than the best memory.

21. Be awake, aware, and curious about everything. You never know what obscure bit of stuff will provide the solution you need.

22. Never take anything for granted.

23. Never neglect or abuse your tools, and always clean up after yourself.

24. Back up your files. Back up the backup.

25. Use Osborn's Checklist:

    1. Put to other uses
    2. Adapt
    3. Modify
    4. Magnify
    5. Minify [sic]
    6. Substitute
    7. Rearrange
    8. Reverse
    9. Combine

26. Speak truthfully and passionately, but courteously (see Rule #33).

27. Dress appropriately for the occasion. Club clothes for the club, beach clothes for the beach, gym clothes for the gym, business clothing for business.

28. Men: Remember that a gentleman always looks a lady in the eyes, no matter what she is wearing.

29. Women: Remember that Ginger Rogers did everything Fred Astaire did, but backwards and in high heels.

30. Remember that the great American author Mark Twain said, "It isn't what we don't know that gives us trouble, it's what we know that ain't so."

31. Have adventures, but avoid the Six Ds of Unintended, Lasting Consequences:

    1. Death
    2. Disease
    3. Dismemberment
    4. Detention
    5. Dependents
    6. Debt

32. When you do something wrong, follow my mother's Four Steps to Forgiveness:

    1. "I did something wrong"
    2. "I'm very sorry."
    3. "I will never do it again."
    4. "How can I make amends?"

    Unfortunately, many people never manage to make it to step one, preferring instead to blame someone else.

33. When speaking, follow these Five Rules of Courteous Discourse. If these simple rules are followed, you can strongly disagree with someone while remaining courteous. If these rules are not followed, then the focus of the conversation changes and the goal of the discussion is not likely to be achieved.

   1. Stick to the subject.
       Limit the discussion to the current topic. "I think your current policy is flawed for these reasons...," is courteous. "This is just like that other time twelve years ago when you were wrong..." is not courteous.

   2. Don't call names.
       Make it a discussion about ideas, not about personalities. "I disagree with your policy," is courteous. "I disagree, you evil bastard/devil/jerk," is not courteous.

   3. Use proper forms of address.
       "Your Majesty/Mr. President/Professor/ Dean, I strongly disagree with your policy," is courteous. "Hey you..." is not courteous.

   4. Don't interrupt.
       Sometimes a moderator is necessary.

   5. Don't raise your voice.
       Being louder often leads to violating courtesy rules 1, 2, 3, and 4. Courtesy is a way of maintaining public control, dignity and self- respect, and it is not the same as just being nice. Rant and swear in private, but maintain your control in public.

34. Know what you think, know what you feel, and know the difference.

35. Don't say "I think" when you are talking about how you feel, and don't say "I feel" when you are talking about what you think. (see Rule #33)

36. Learn more and keep learning. The more you learn, the more you become capable of learning.

37. Be kind and generous.

38. Add your own rules.

39. It is up to you.

think.

   feel.

      say.

         do.

            make the world better.

Glossary

? = ABC

Glossary

A/B Testing – Incoming

When website visitor traffic is directed equally to two versions of a website design and each site visitor sees only one version of the site. Each visitor's interaction with the site is tracked and evaluated, and the most effective site design is then used as the final version.

A/B Testing – Outgoing

For email subject line testing, a smaller test sample of a final email list is selected. This sample group is split into two, with each half receiving an email with only one version of the subject line. The version that is opened most, and has the most click-throughs, and ultimately the best conversion, will then be applied to the entire email list for deployment.

Account Management

The agency employees who are the client's representative to the agency, and also the agency's voice to the client. Account Management also refers to the process by which these objectives are accomplished.

Account Planning

The agency employees who are the representatives of the client's customers to the agency. Account planners fulfill this role by providing relevant strategic insights into the essential motivations of a client's current and potential customers, and developing a plan for the account based on this understanding.

Agency-of-Record

The traditional model of agency business, where the agency is under an agreement to be the primary or sole partner of a client company for the purposes of developing creative marketing communications and media placement. The AOR model has largely shifted to that of a Lead Agency that continues to be a primary business partner and brand steward while coordinating their efforts with other specialist agencies.

Art Director

An agency employee or freelancer who concepts and designs visual communications for a variety of media. They may also direct graphic designers, illustrators, photographers, and other specialist visual creators as needed. The Art Director is traditionally partnered with a Copywriter.

Attribution

Determining which exposure to a specific piece of marketing communications had the effect of moving a specific consumer to take action.

Big Idea

The unifying creative concept that drives the marketing communication efforts of a brand, product, or service.

Brain Dump

The first step of a Brainstorm in which the participants suggest the ideas they had in response to reading the background information prior to the Brainstorm session.

Brainstorming
The name given to methods of creative idea generation by a group in order to solve a problem.

Brand Attitude Funnel
A renamed and new application of the traditional linear Purchase Funnel model, which is outdated with respect to the complexity of contemporary consumer actions and decisions.

Business-to-Business (B2B)
All marketing and marketing communications directed at businesses that use the products or services of the agency's client company in the operations of their business.

Business-to-Consumer (B2C)
All marketing and marketing communications directed at potential customers of the products or services of the agency's client company.

Business-to-Trade Channel (B2T)
All marketing and marketing communications directed at businesses that resell the products or services of the agency's client company.

Call to Action
Marketing ommunications content intended to pursuade the viewer to perform a specific action, such as clicking on a link, visiting a website, going to a store, or purchasing a product.

Check Bid
When a company has a bidding process in place that requires a certain minimum number of agencies to bid on the work, and there is an incumbent agency who is virtually guaranteed to win the account. The other agencies are only asked to bid for the purpose of fulfilling the number of bidders required by the company process. Agencies comply with these requests with the hopes that they will be included in the bidding for future opportunities that they may actually win.

Comprehensive Layout (Comp)
A visual representation of proposed marketing communications that is rendered to closely resemble the finished product.

Content Marketing
A strategic marketing approach that focuses on creating and distributing valuable, relevant, and consistent content to attract and retain a clearly defined audience and ultimately to drive profitable customer interaction

Conversion
Getting webite visitors to perform a desired action, such as purchase, enrollment, or providing contact information.

Copywriter
An agency employee or freelancer who concepts and creates written communications across a broad range of applications for a variety of media. The Copywriter is often partnered with an Art Director.

Cost-Plus Pricing
A pricing scheme that sets a billable rate per hour of work by agency employees, multiplies this rate times the hours required to accomplish a given task, then adds a percentage for profit.

Creative Brief
A document containing essential information and actionable audience insights that enables the creation of effective solutions by the Creative Team.

Creative Director
An agency employee or freelancer who supervises Creative teams, and is responsible for concepting and also approving the work of the Creative teams.

Creative Process
The steps followed by Creatives to consistently achieve unique and effective results. Learning and mastering the Creative Process is a principal objective of creative education for aspiring designers and copywriters.

Creative Rationale
The explanation of how a proposed Creative execution delivers effective solutions and will achieve defined objectives.

Creative Strategy.
The Promotion aspect of the 4 Ps of marketing encompasses Creative strategy. Creative strategy includes the "Big Idea," the unifying, innovative concept that drives the marketing efforts of a brand or product.

Day-Rate Pricing
A pricing scheme that sets a billable rate per hour of work by agency employees; this rate is then multiplied times eight hours. A half-day rate is typically for five hours at the eight hour rate.

Degree of Difficulty Multiplier
When the client and/or any intermediary person within the agency complicates the process by their involvement, the estimated number of hours is increased proportionally.

Demographics
The relevant attributes of the potential customers of a company including age, gender, marital status, educational status, and household income.

Direct Marketing
Data-driven, multichannel marketing communications targeted directly at specific potential customers of a company, rather than through an intermediary media channel.

Directional Verbs
Signified by arrows in Tactical Integration Mapping to represent the intended action taken by the recipient of the communication.

Double Employee Rate Pricing
A rule-of-thumb pricing scheme used by freelancers, in which the hourly rate of an agency employee is doubled to cover costs of doing business.

Elements of Design

The building blocks of design, including dot, line, shape, form, space, color, texture, and motion.

Evaluation

The assessment of the performance of campaign executions with respect to the objectives.

Focus Groups

A Qualitative Research technique in which a select number of people are assembled in a room, directed in a discussion by a moderator, and usually observed and recorded through one-way glass by a team of researchers.

Folder of Unsent Rants

A physical or digital folder wherein is stored letters, memos, and/or emails that were written in anger and prudently not sent.

For Position Only (FPO)

A placeholder image in a layout that will not be used in the final work.

Geographics

The relevant location information about a company's potential customers.

Gestalt Principles

Design principles that include grouping by similarity, grouping by proximity, continuity, closure, equilibrium, and common fate.

Greeking

Using placeholder text composed of nonsense words or Latin to show the correct typeface usage in a layout but not the final wording. Greeking refers both to the process of placing the type ("I'm Greeking the type in this layout."), and to the nonsense text itself ("The Greeking is set in 10 point Helvetica.").

Hairy Arms

One term for a method employed by creatives to avoid excessive changes to their work, by providing their supervisor with an obvious mistake to correct. This is based on a story that Disney animators would add hair to the arms of character concepts so that their studio bosses would have something to critique, and would then leave the rest of their concepts unchanged.

Idea Book

A small, easily carried book for recording ideas, observations, inspirations, sketches, and notes.

Impression

A person's exposure to an example of marketing communications on one occasion.

Inverted Pyramid

A writing structure used by journalists and press release writers for prioritizing and presenting information.

Island of Orphan Ideas

A physical and digital file folder of ideas that never got used. See **Unpublished Concepts.**

Jargon
Words or phrases unique to a specific profession or group.

Job Method Pricing
A pricing scheme in which a total, "flat rate" price for the work is given, without providing details of the hours required.

Job Number
An agency reference number assigned to each project for the purposes of accurate accounting and billing.

Key Performance Indicator (KPI)
A measurable value of key business objectives. Often referred to as a metric.

Lead Generation
The process of researching and collecting the names and contact information of potential customers of a company.

Lede
The introductory paragraph of a story, article, or essay.

Marketing Strategy
The result of the application of the traditional "4 Ps" — Price, Place, Product, Promotion — being applied, individually and together, particularly as an outgrowth of a SWOT.

Measurement
The collection of actual performance data of each tactical execution, such as, for example, the return rate (in numbers) of a piece of direct marketing (tactical execution).

Media Buyer
An agency employee or freelancer who negotiates prices and time slots with a media company for the placement of advertising.

Media Department
The agency department that researches, plans, and contracts with a media company to show advertising and marketing communications where the intended audience will be most likely to see, interact with, and remember it.

Media Planner
An agency employee or freelancer who identifies which specific media platforms and companies will be most effective for the placement of advertising on behalf of the agency's clients.

Memory Palace
A visualization tool for sorting and retrieving information from memory, in which each type of information is stored in a particular drawer in a particular piece of furniture in a specific room, within a mental image of a building.

Microaggressions
Casual interpersonal insults and slights directed at members of one group by a person of another group.

Multivariate Testing
Similar to A/B testing where only two variables are tested, but compares a larger number of variables to test how these elements interact in context.

Nodes

Signified by the circles used in Tactical Integration Mapping to represent each participating communicator.

Nouns

Signified by the rectangles used in Tactical Integration Mapping to represent each specific marketing communication.

Osborn's Checklist

A list of keywords applied to provoke original thinking in creative problem solving.

Othering

Treating a person or group of people as different, alien, or not one of "us" (they are the "others")

Out of Scope

Additional services not specified in the Start of Work Agreement.

Paid Search

An agreement in which a company pays fees to have high-ranking placement in search engine results.

Parking Lot

A specified area of a whiteboard or a designated sheet of flipchart paper used during a Brainstorm for recording ideas with potential that are off topic or out of sequence so that the ideas will not be forgotten. The same technique can be used by an individual while taking notes during a meeting or brainstorm session.

Primary Objectives

The objectives of an overall IMC campaign or program, as distinguished from the objectives of each individual tactic (referred to as tactical objectives) used in that campaign or program.

Principles of Design

Describes how the elements of design are used, including balance, emphasis, movement, proportion, pattern, rhythm, unity, variety, and the Gestalt principles.

Process Book

A binder into which everything related to a course is placed, including the syllabus, class notes, research, concepts, rough drafts, digital backup and archive copies, and finished work.

Production Timeline

Defines deadlines for project work, including intermediate and final deadlines.

Project Change Notification (PCN)

A document describing the additional services requested by a client beyond those covered in the original Scope of Work, and the associated fees required to complete those services.

Project Post Mortem

An evaluation meeting following the conclusion of a project, wherein the project process is examined for successes to be repeated, and flaws to be corrected.

Psychographics

The attitudes, interests, activities, opinions, and aspirations of current and potential customers.

Purchase Funnel

A traditional linear model of consumer actions; it is now outdated with respect to the complexity of contemporary consumer actions and decision making.

Qualitative Research Methods

Methods that result in information about the thoughts and feelings of members of the target audience.

Quantitative Research Methods

Methods based on objective measurements and numerical analysis of data.

Question Reluctance

Hesitation about asking a question, often due to shyness, language problems, embarrassment, or the belief that the answer should already be known.

Radding's Law

Dictates that given a choice of options, the client is most likely to pick the worst one

Jarrell's Corollary to Radding's Law:

Dictates that the most minor problems produce the greatest number of negative customer comments.

Lloyd's Corollary to Radding's Law:

Dictates that if the worst option is also the most expensive, the likelihood that the client will choose this option is reduced.

Red Herring

Something that is meant to be misleading.

Request for Proposal (RFP)

A solicitation by a company to an agency requesting that the agency propose services they would provide to the company, and the fees associated with these services.

Request for Quotation (RFQ)

A company requesting that an agency state the fees they would charge for services specified in the request.

Return on Marketing Investment (ROMI)

A method for calculating the financial effectiveness of an advertising or marketing activity. The basic formula for this calculation is

$$\frac{\text{Gross Profit} - \text{Marketing Investment}}{\text{Marketing Investment}} = \text{ROMI}$$

Scope Creep

When an agency accepts requests for additional work on a project without charging additional fees.

Scope of Work

The services and products that the agency will deliver for the fees charged.

Search Engine Optimization (SEO)

Methods to increase the number of visitors to a website by achieving high-ranking placement on the results pages of search engines.

Selling to the Brief

Presenting a Creative Rationale to a client that explains how the proposed creative solution delivers on the objectives specified in the Creative Brief.

Social Media Manager
An agency employee or freelancer who develops strategy, plans, and content; manages content placement on relevant social media channels; and monitors the effectiveness of those choices.

Spec Work
Short for Speculative Work, any finished Creative work that is presented to the client before the agency or freelancer receives compensation.

Start of Work Agreement
Encompasses the Scope of Work, plus the schedule and agreement about additional fees for work not included in the Scope of Work document.

Stickiness
The quality of a website that encourages site visitors to remain on that site for a longer time.

Strategy
A concept of how business goals can be achieved.

SWOT Analysis
An analysis of the Strengths, Weaknesses, Opportunities, and Threats in the marketplace.

Tactical Integration Mapping
A technique of graphic visualization of the interactions, measurements, analytics, and tracking for the planning and evaluation of marketing communications campaign component effectiveness.

Tactical Objective
The goal of each marketing communication tactic, such as advertising or direct mail. Tactics work together in a connected chain of effects to achieve the Primary Objectives of the overall campaign or program.

Tactics
Actions undertaken to execute a strategy.

Task Method Pricing
A pricing scheme that looks at the time required to accomplish each small task, applies an hourly rate to the time for each task, then totals these task amounts to arrive at the price charged for the finished work.

10X Rule
Principle stating that increasing relative cost of changes at each stage of creative development and production is approximately ten times the cost of a change at the previous stage.

Time Tracking
Accounting for time spent on a particular job or account.

To Do List
An enumerated, prioritized listing of tasks to be accomplished

Unique Value Proposition (UVP) or Unique Sales Proposition (USP)
A statement of what a company or product offers in the marketplace that is different, distinct, and of worth to consumers.

Unpublished Concepts
Ideas that were not selected for use by a client, but that have merit as a example in your portfolio of work. See **Island of Orphan Ideas**.

Voice
A distinct brand personality expressed through a particular style of copy or visual imagery.

Webinar
A seminar delivered via the internet.

White Paper
A response to an RFP that includes strategy, staff profiles, examples of previous work, and budget. Often called a white paper because this response is a text-only document with limited formatting and no graphics.

Work Order
A document used to initiate simple tactical work; request updates or changes; or specify simple extensions of previously developed work into additional versions.

Additional Reading

1. ABC

2. DEF

3. GHI

4. JKL

5. MNO

Additional Reading

An eclectic list covering a wide range of useful topics

History and Culture

Diamond, Jared (2005). *Guns, Germs, and Steel: The Fates of Human Societies.* New York: W. W. Norton & Company.

Gordon, Stewart. (2007). *When Asia Was the World.* Boston, MA: Da Capo Press.

Hirsch, E. D.; Kett, Joseph F.; Trefil, James. (2002). *The New Dictionary of Cultural Literacy: What Every American Needs to Know.* Boston, MA: Houghton Mifflin Harcourt; Revised ed.

Jones, Terry (1985). *Chaucer's Knight: The Portrait of a Medieval Mercenary.* London: Methuen; Revised ed.

Loewen, James W. (2008). *Lies My Teacher Told Me (Everything Your American History Textbook Got Wrong, Completely Revised and Updated).* New York: The New Press; 2nd ed.

Rhetoric and Logic

Baillargeon, Normand. (2008). *A Short Course in Intellectual Self-Defense.* New York: Seven Stories Press.

Hall, Sean. (2007). *This Means This, This Means That: A User's Guide to Semiotics.* London: Laurence King Publishers.

Advertising and Marketing

Godin, Seth. (2009). *All Marketers are Liars: The Underground Classic That Explains How Marketing Really Works--and Why Authenticity Is the Best Marketing of All.* New York: Portfolio.

Kelley, Larry D.; Sheehan, Kim Bartel. (2017). *Advertising Strategy: A 360 Degree Brand Approach.* Irvine, CA; Melvin & Leigh.

McGinniss, Joe. (1988) *The Selling of the President.* New York: Penguin; Reprint ed.

McKee, Steve. (2007). *Beware the Advertising Pretest.* Retrieved from http://www.bloomberg.com/news/articles/2007-12-07/beware-the-advertising-pretestbusinessweek-business-news-stock-market-and-financial-advice

Ogilvy, David Ogilvy. (1985). *Ogilvy on Advertising.* New York: Vintage. Vintage Books Edition.

Design

Buxton, Bill. (2007). *Sketching User Experiences: Getting the Design Right and the Right Design.* Burlington, MA: Morgan Kaufmann.

Frease, Jessica. (2014). Transcript from "All Things Considered." Retrieved from http://www.npr.org/2014/11/17/364760847/whats-with-all-of-the-hairy-arms-in-graphic-design (original work broadcast November 17, 2014).

Lidwell, William; Holden, Kritina; Butler, Jill. (2010). *Universal Principles of Design, Revised and Updated: 125 Ways to Enhance Usability, Influence Perception, Increase Appeal, Make Better Design Decisions, and Teach through Design.* Beverly, MA: Rockport Publishers, 2nd ed.

Nelms, Henning. (1986). *Thinking with a Pencil.* Berkeley, CA: Ten Speed Press. Reprint Edition.

Tufte, Edward R. (2001). *The Visual Display of Quantitative Information.* Cheshire, CT: Graphics Press; 2nd ed.

Philosophy

Lao Tzu (2006). *Tao Te Ching: A New English Version* (S. Mitchell, Trans.) New York: Harper Perennial Modern Classics; (Original work 4th century BCE)

Loewer, Barry. (2009). *30-Second Philosophies: The 50 Most Thought-Provoking Philosophies, Each Explained in Half A Minute.* New York: Fall River Press.

Machiavelli, Nicolo (1984) *The Prince* (D. Donno, Trans.) New York: Bantam Classics. (Original work published 1532).

Miyamoto Musashi. (2002). *The Book of Five Rings* (W. S. Wilson, Trans.) Tokyo, Japan: Kodansha International (Original work circa 1645)

Pirsig, Robert M. (2008). *Zen and the Art of Motorcycle Maintenance: An Inquiry into Values.* New York: Harper Perennial Modern Classics (Originally published 1974)

Sun Tzu. (1971). *The Art of War* (S.B. Griffith, Trans.). Oxford, UK: Oxford University Press (Original work 5th century BCE)

Novels

Bradbury, Ray. (1952) *A Sound of Thunder.* Springfield, OH: Crowell-Collier.

Doyle, Arthur Conan (2009). *The Complete Sherlock Holmes. New York:* Barnes & Noble. (Originally publshed 1887–1927)

Ellison, Ralph. (1995). *Invisible Man.* New York: Vintage Books; 2nd edition (Originally published 1952)

Heller, Joseph. (1996). *Catch-22.* New York: Simon & Schuster. Reprint Edition.

Huxley, Aldous. (2006). *Brave New World.* New York: Harper Perennia. (Reprint edition).

Orwell, George. (1961). *1984.* New York: New American Library.

Simmons, Dan. (1989). *Hyperion (Hyperion Cantos, Book 1).* New York: Doubleday.

Vonnegut, Kurt. (1999). *Slaughterhouse-Five: A Novel.* New York: Dial Press; Reissue edition (Originally published 1969)

Thinking, Creativity, Connection, Process

Buzan, T. & Buzan, B. (1996). *The Mind Map Book: How to Use Radiant Thinking to Maximize Your Brain's Untapped Potential.* New York: Plume. Reprint Edition.

Carnegie, Dale. (1998). *How to Win Friends & Influence People.* New York: Gallery Books. Reprint Edition.

Cheng, Karen. (2012) *How to Survive a Critique: A Guide to Giving and Receiving Feedback.* Retrieved from http://www.aiga.org/how-to-survive-a-critique/

Covey, Stephen R. (2013). *The 7 Habits of Highly Effective People: Powerful Lessons in Personal Change.* New York: Simon & Schuster; Anniversary edition.

Csikszentmihalyi, Mihaly. (1997). *Creativity: Flow and the Psychology of Discovery and Invention.* New York: Harper Perennial.

Csikszentmihalyi, Mihaly (2008). *Flow: The Psychology of Optimal Experience.* New York: Harper Perennial.

Guildford, J. P. (1967). *The Nature of Human Intelligence.* New York: McGraw-Hill.

Jaffe, Eric. (2015). "Morning People vs. Night Owls: 9 Insights Backed By Science." Retrieved from www.fastcodesign.com/3046391/evidence/morning-people-vs-night-people-9-insights-backed-by-science

Kaplan, Abraham. (1964). *The Conduct of Inquiry: Methodology for Behavioral Science* (p. 28). San Francisco, CA: Chandler.

Lilly, John C. (1987). *Programming and Metaprogramming in the Human Biocomputer: Theory and Experiments.* New York: Three Rivers Press; 2nd ed.

Lorenz, Edward. (1972, December). Transcript of speech presented at the American Association for the Advancement of Science. Retrieved from http://eaps4.mit.edu/research/Lorenz/Butterfly_1972.pdf

Maslow, Abraham H. (1969). *Psychology of Science: A Reconnaissance* (p. 15). Washington, D.C.: Gateway Editions.

Mencken, H. L. (1926, September 19). "Notes on Journalism." *The Chicago Tribune.* Retrieved from http://archives.chicagotribune.com/1926/09/19/page/87/article/notes-on-journalism

Osborn, Alex. (1953). *Applied Imagination: Principles and Procedures of Creative Problem Solving.* New York: Charles Scribner's Sons.

Sparks, Sarah D. (2014, August 19). *Students' Help-Seeking Strategies Offer Clues for Educators.* Retrieved from http://www.edweek.org/ew/articles/2014/08/20/01help.h34.html

Sue, Derald Wing. (2010). "Racial Microaggressions in Everyday Life." Retrieved from www.psychologytoday.com/blog/microaggressions-in-everyday-life/201010/racial-microaggressions-in-everyday-life

Theibert, Philip R. (1997). *How to Give a Damn Good Speech.* Wayne, NJ: Career Press.

Index

Index

Colophon

The typefaces used in this book are Gotham and Futura.

The chapter title pages are set in Futura Bold.
The page headings are Futura Medium.

The body copy is Gotham Book.
The body subheadings are Gotham Bold.

The body copy for problem stories is Futura Medium Oblique.
The footnotes are Futura Book Oblique.

The page layout is based on a 5 x 7 modular grid inside the page margins, with 0.125" vertical alleys between columns and 0.125" horizontal spaces between rows.

About the Author

Joseph B. Radding is a brand storyteller, educator, consultant, integrated brand and marketing communications director, creative director, art director and graphic designer, brainstorm facilitator, presentation coach, painter, actor, photographer, writer, mentor, manager, and speaker,

Joe is available to speak and conduct workshops based on the content of this book and other related subjects.

He lives in Michigan with his wife Marilee and their cats Bella and Chaucer.